D1498636

START HERE

DON WILLIAMS

Regal

From Gospel Light
Ventura, California, U.S.A.

PUBLISHED BY REGAL BOOKS
FROM GOSPEL LIGHT
VENTURA, CALIFORNIA, U.S.A.
PRINTED IN THE U.S.A.

Regal

Regal Books is a ministry of Gospel Light, a Christian publisher dedicated to serving the local church. We believe God's vision for Gospel Light is to provide church leaders with biblical, user-friendly materials that will help them evangelize, disciple and minister to children, youth and families.

It is our prayer that this Regal book will help you discover biblical truth for your own life and help you meet the needs of others. May God richly bless you.

For a free catalog of resources from Regal Books/Gospel Light, please call your Christian supplier or contact us at 1-800-4-GOSPEL *or* www.regalbooks.com.

Library of Congress Cataloging-in-Publication Data
Williams, Don, 1937-
    Start here / by Don Williams.
        p. cm.
    ISBN 0-8307-4297-2 (trade paper)
    1. Christian life. 2. Sanctification. 3. Spiritual formation. I. Title.
    BV4501.3.W551 2006
    248.4—dc22   2006022409

1   2   3   4   5   6   7   8   9   10   /   10   09   08   07   06

Rights for publishing this book in other languages are contracted by Gospel Light Worldwide, the international nonprofit ministry of Gospel Light. Gospel Light Worldwide also provides publishing and technical assistance to international publishers dedicated to producing Sunday School and Vacation Bible School curricula and books in the languages of the world. For additional information, visit www.gospellightworldwide.org; write to Gospel Light Worldwide, P.O. Box 3875, Ventura, CA 93006; or send an e-mail to info@gospellightworldwide.org.

DEDICATION

*For Roger Batchelder, Adam Campbell, Mike Parker and
Philip Winchester, my band of brothers.*

CONTENTS

Author's Note

Having been in professional ministry for more than 40 years, I have lost track of some literary documentation for a few references in this text. Other citations come out of the oral tradition. This is especially true for quotes from John Wimber and Francis MacNutt, who have spoken again and again into my life, but it also includes a few others who have said a pithy or directive word to me.

Most of the references here are documented with appropriate footnotes, but I have chosen to include some quotations without documentation whose absence would weaken this book. These quotations are not especially scholarly in content, but are more of a collected "wisdom literature" and have pastoral impact. These "seasonable" words have stuck with me over the years and will continue to build the Church as an instrument of the Kingdom. After all, this is what we are about.

The title of chapter 3, "Here I Am to Worship" is the title of Tim Hughes's Dove Award-winning song, which has gone worldwide. As a dear friend, I take the liberty of borrowing it from him.

CHAPTER 1

WHAT'S HAPPENED TO ME?

You may have gone forward at a Billy Graham rally and accepted Christ. You may have responded to an invitation at the end of a morning service. You may have prayed with a Sunday School teacher or parent years ago. You may have listened to a TV evangelist's appeal or read a tract such as the "Four Spiritual Laws" and prayed the sinner's prayer. You may have made a decision at a summer camp, or Jesus may have met you in a desperate hour as you cried out to Him. But what exactly happened at that moment? You were delivered from Satan's kingdom and catapulted into the kingdom of God.

At the time this occurred, you probably had no idea that this was actually happening. It might even sound foreign to you now. Often, the gospel is presented simply as asking Jesus into our hearts, having our sins forgiven and receiving the assurance that were we to die tonight, we would "go to heaven." The Christian life is then spelled out as reading our Bible, learning to pray, finding a church where Christ is preached and sharing our faith with others. But conversion includes much more than this. The apostle Paul wrote to the Colossians that they had been transferred from the kingdom of darkness into the kingdom of God's Beloved Son (see Col. 1:13).

When Jesus began His public ministry, He announced that the kingdom of God was within reach and called His listeners to repent and believe in the good news (see Mark 1:15). Later, He said that the kingdom of God was in their midst (see Luke 11:20). He was the King and had come to bring God's reign into their history and into their hearts. He does the same today. When we submit to Him, He enters in by His Spirit. Our conversion immediately depletes the population of Satan's kingdom by one as our little stories become a part of Jesus' big story, and we now participate in His purpose to re-establish God's reign throughout the universe.

Two problems must be solved for us to become Christians. First, we must be delivered from Satan's kingdom. Second, we must be delivered from God's wrath. But for many people today, these two problems are almost incomprehensible. Let me sketch it out.

DELIVERANCE FROM SATAN'S KINGDOM

The whole world system is under the rule of a powerful, supernatural being that hates God, hates all goodness, hates all absolutes (apart from his absolute evil) and hates you and me (see 1 John 5:19). He is God's unequivocal enemy. Once a great heavenly angel, Satan rebelled against God's kingdom in order to establish his own. He now hides behind our perceptions of reality (worldviews), assumptions, values and the political and religious systems of this fallen world order. He lies to us about our value and worth, the meaning and purpose of life, and our ultimate destiny. Often, he uses the arts and the media to warp our sense of reality and to turn us away from God. He thrusts other, false gods (idols) before us and seduces us into worshiping them, even to the point of addiction. He disguises himself as an "angel of light" (2 Cor. 11:14). He manipulates our instincts—to eat, to not be eaten and to reproduce[1]—and our insecurities in order to market his false ideology and the promises and products of his kingdom.

The deepest emptiness in our lives—the hole in our souls—is the absence of God. Satan promises that we can fill that hole with substances, activities, products and people. Yet the truth is that we are made for God, and without His life in us, we will remain spiritually dead and eternally lonely. In all creation, those beings closest to God are people. We have been made to love God and to love each other as ourselves. But apart from God, people become idols, too. We become codependent and addicted to each other, which ultimately perverts every relationship. In turn, this becomes an inroad for demonic assault, which ends up in death. Satan deceives us in order to kill us. He wants us to share in his doom, because he hates us and the God who loves us and made us in His image.

Over the entry gate to the Nazi concentration camp Auschwitz, a sign in wrought iron letters reads, "Arbeit Macht Frei," which translates, "Work Makes You Free." Untold numbers of Jews and others saw this promise as they entered the camp, only to find it was a total lie. There was no freedom there, only death in the gas chambers. Likewise, Satan lifts up his signs over the gates of our prison as we roll into his gas chambers: "You can be your own god" or "Go ahead and have some fun now—you can worry about God later" or "Put yourself first! Who else is going to look after your interests?" The devil continually pounds on us to grab more, consume more and collect more. He promises to satisfy us with quick and bogus fixes that will feed our egos, our insecurities and the ache inside. But when those fixes wear off, there is always the morning after. As we go through withdrawals, loss and grief, we sink into depression, anger turned inward, and "buyer's remorse"—the pain of realizing that the new hookup, pickup, job advancement or whatever never satisfies for long.

Again and again, Satan lifts up signs along the road to his gas chamber—signs that promise us freedom from the cycle of pain and shame. But there is only one true banner: "Christ Is Freedom" (see John 8:31-32). The devil wants to block this truth from our minds so that we remain docile, drugged, obedient, fantasy-fed, fantasy-led and addicted subjects of his doomed kingdom.

DELIVERANCE FROM GOD'S WRATH

If it is hard for some of us to believe in Satan's kingdom; it is even harder to believe in God's kingdom, a kingdom of justice ruled by a just King. God is just. He judges our moral failure—which He calls "sin"—and will separate Himself and His people from unrepentant sinners for eternity. One day, He will clean house and totally rule His universe again. Why does this seem to be so far off our radar screens?

First of all, in our postmodern world, few people believe in moral absolutes anymore. We are told that they make us narrow, judgmental and intolerant of others, their religious convictions and their lifestyles. Our inherited philosophy is to live and let live. We are told that each person has his or her own truth and that the ultimate goal for eve ryone ought to be open-mindedness. But as professor Allan Bloom once wrote, "To look into an open mind is to look into an empty mind; nothing is there."[2]

While many in our culture champion moral relativism, none of us can actually live that way. Very few people could tolerate living in a society without rules. Without absolutes, there would be no Constitution or Bill of Rights, no laws, no justice, no police, no contracts, no partnerships, no corporations, no marriages. We would live the law of the jungle.

Without absolutes, we could lie, steal and murder without consequences. We could be racists, fascists or anarchists. Our courts would collapse due to the lack of any absolute standard of justice, and we would collapse along with them—our identities fragmented and our mental health shattered. Without absolutes, we would be ravaged by addictions, trying to fill the holes in our souls, with our passions controlling us rather than us controlling them.

Without absolutes, we would have no personal boundaries or moral structure for life. We would have no way to tell our children what is right or wrong. Did you beat up your sister? That's your "truth." Did you have sex with your brother, your child, your dog? That's your "truth." The absence of absolutes leads logically to insanity and suicide.

Without an absolute standard of justice, democracy would be impossible. Truth, accountability and public trust would all go down the drain. There would be no basis for moral outrage over Third World debt, poverty or the AIDS pandemic. Growing opium in Afghanistan or cocaine in Columbia? No problem! That's your "truth." Building reactors for nuclear bombs? No problem. That's an internal matter, not a matter for the United Nations or the community of nations. Polluting the atmosphere? Increasing global warming? No big deal. No absolutes means no commitment to the next generation or to the preservation of the earth.

C. S. Lewis argued that our innate sense of right and wrong is reflected by our offense at someone breaking into line at the drinking fountain or our refusal to give a medal to a soldier for running away from battle.[3] God's moral law is written on our hearts, despite how relative our cultural morals have become. God is completely just, and not only do His laws reveal His just character, but also living by them makes life possible in a sick and fallen world.

The second reason why we are asleep to the reality of God's justice and judgment is because we've been told that *if* God exists, He is merely a benign spirit who would never judge anyone or send him or her to hell. He is the Great Therapist, committed to rebuilding our low self-esteem. But however this reassuring image may be, the life and death question is not, "Is our concept of God pleasant, agreeable or comforting?" but, "Is it true?"

It has often been said that we expect more justice from the sheriff than we do from God. We are offended when criminals go free because we believe that crimes must be punished and justice must be served. When the police officers accused of assaulting Rodney King were acquitted by a mostly white jury in 1992, many people felt justice had not been done, especially since the brutal beating of King was captured on videotape for the world to see. Likewise, many people found it hard to believe that O. J. Simpson walked on a double-murder charge. It is hard to forget the TV images of him fleeing the law in the back of a Ford Bronco with his passport, thousands of dollars in cash, and a false beard.

If we demand human justice in this life, how much more should we demand divine justice? Will history's mass murderers escape? The answer is no. Even if they commit suicide like Hitler in his bunker or die of old age like Stalin, they must face the bar of God. There is a Day of Judgment coming in which divine justice and the human cry for justice will meet and be satisfied.

While most of us are not murderous tyrants like Hitler, Stalin, Pol Pot or Osama bin Laden, *we are all sinners*. Despite our rationalizations and excuses, we too deserve God's judgment, His divine wrath. Not only have we failed to measure up to His absolute standard—in intention if not in action (see Matt. 5)—we have failed to measure up to our own standard. Every time we lie, gossip, withhold the truth, shade the facts or tell people what they want to hear rather than what we know or believe to be the truth, we violate our own conscience. We violate the law of God written on our hearts.

Therefore, because God is perfect in His moral character and righteous in His judgments, we stand condemned both before Him and our own consciences. We deserve His wrath for our sin—our fundamental failure to worship, honor and serve Him as God. We have substituted ourselves for Him, making our needs, wants, lusts, philosophies, fantasies and drives the worship center of our lives. We either worship God or we worship idols, and the most available and pervasive idol is ourself. Our basic question is, "What's in it for me?" instead of, "What's in it for God and others?"

If we need deliverance from Satan's kingdom, then we also need deliverance from God's wrath. His holy anger is the consequence of His justice, which stands against our sin and finds us guilty of rebellion, selfishness and idolatry. We desperately need deliverance, because life is short and we will soon appear before God's judgment seat on the other side of death.

DELIVERANCE INTO GOD'S KINGDOM

Now we are ready for the most outrageous and surprising good news of all: The kingdom of God is within reach! God is establishing His justice and sovereign rule in this world to uphold His law and forgive, receive and transform sinners. His kingdom comes, however, not as a result of a divine ego trip, but rather through humble sacrifice and self-giving love. It turns our values upside down.

For the kingdom of God to fully come, Jesus had to become the suffering servant of the Lord. According to Isaiah 53, He took the place of sinners, satisfied divine justice, and died the death we all deserved for our sins. As the Lamb of God who takes away the sins of the world, Jesus went freely and resolutely to Jerusalem to sacrifice Himself on the cross. Because He was both human and divine, as a human He died a real and bloody death, while as a divine being He paid an immeasurable price for the garbage pile of sin dumped by the human race.

In the death of Jesus, God's justice was satisfied (upheld), the moral and legal debt of all our sin was paid in full, and God's mercy was extended to each of us. He didn't quit being a God of wrath and suddenly become a God of love; He has loved us continually from all eternity. But the ground on which He could accept us was dramatically changed. The penalty for sin was paid, and all who have faith in Jesus are freely and fully justified (see Rom. 3:26). At the cross, God lifted His wrath from us and placed it upon Himself through His Son. The death we deserve to die He died for us in our place. All we can do in response is to lay down our arms, humble ourselves and receive His acceptance by faith alone.

Martin Luther said that to become a Christian is like being married. When we are wedded to Christ by faith, we give Him all we have and He gives us all He has. We give Him all our sins, and He gives us all His righteousness.[4] We are now righteous before God through the righteousness of His Son.

When we ask Jesus to forgive us, we enter God's kingdom through the gate marked "Justice Satisfied, Mercy Granted." God's reign is set up in our hearts. But there is more! When we come to Christ, we are not only delivered from Satan's kingdom but are also delivered into God's kingdom. When we come to Christ, He zips us open and jumps inside. We are raised to a new life. Let's look next at what that means.

CHAPTER 2

DELIVERED INTO GOD'S KINGDOM

Many evangelists stress accepting Jesus for forgiveness of sins, assurance of salvation and eternal life, and then leave it at that. But even more fundamental is the *exchange of sovereignties*. We either live in Satan's counterfeit kingdom of darkness or we live in the kingdom of God.

Paul told the Corinthians that if the gospel is veiled, it is because Satan has blinded the minds of the unbelievers to keep them from seeing "the light of the gospel of the glory of Christ" (2 Cor. 4:4). But when we confess that Jesus is Lord, God takes off our blinders and we are able to see. Now we are in His kingdom. But what does this mean?

SUBMISSION

First, entering God's kingdom means submitting to the King. When we call Jesus "Lord," we use the very name given to God in the Old Testament and surrender ourselves to Him. Paul makes this confession central to Kingdom life:

"The word is near you, it is in your mouth and in your heart," that is, the word of faith we are proclaiming: that if you confess with your mouth, "Jesus is Lord," and believe in your heart that God raised him from the dead, you will be saved (Rom. 10:8-9).

Jesus is both our living Lord and our risen Savior. As we surrender to Him, we anticipate the day when every knee will bow and every tongue confess that Jesus is Lord to the glory of God the Father (see Phil. 2:11).

Our confession that Jesus is Lord doesn't come from our own insight or inspiration. It comes from His self-revelation, authored by the Father and given through the Spirit. When Peter announced that Jesus was the Christ, the Son of the living God, Jesus didn't congratulate him for his theological acumen or spiritual sensitivity. He called Peter blessed because flesh and blood did not reveal this to him, "But my Father in heaven" (Matt. 16:16). Likewise, Paul told the Corinthians that no one can say Jesus is Lord apart from the Holy Spirit (see 1 Cor. 12:3).

In this same way, our confession of Jesus' lordship comes through the revelation and the conviction of God's Spirit as we enter His kingdom. God speaks for Himself, and He opens our eyes to see and surrender to Him.[1]

To say, "Jesus is Lord" means to renounce all other lords. No ideology, political philosophy, drug or person can have a higher claim on our lives. All our idols must be pulled down, repented of and crushed at Jesus' feet. The idols of pride, power, control, self-medication, family, friends, illicit sex, Internet pornography, legalism, self-righteousness, mind-altering meditation, witchcraft, magic, cults, money, gambling, work, self-advancement, children, health, and security in old age must go. Anything that takes the place of Jesus in our hearts, in our passions and in our devotion is an idol. As Elijah the prophet said to the nation of Israel, "How long will you waver between two opinions? If the Lord is God, follow him" (1 Kings 18:21). God has called us and revealed Jesus as Lord to us. Follow Him!

To say "Jesus is Lord" is to worship Him. The main Hebrew word used in the Bible for "worship" is *shachah*, which means to fall down, to lie prostrate. Paul urged Christians to offer their bodies as "living sacrifices" as a response to God's mercies; this is our "spiritual act of worship" (Rom. 12:1). Paul knew that if God has our bodies—into which are integrated our minds, memories, emotions, desires, instincts, fantasies and will—*He has us*. Beware asking Jesus into your heart with reservations. Withhold nothing from Him—He already owns it all, but He gives us the freedom to give it all back to Him. God doesn't just want our "souls"; He wants it all! Turning our whole selves over to Him is the only way we can escape the diseased instincts and tainted lusts that vie to rule our lives.

We enter the kingdom of God by confessing Jesus as Lord and submitting to Him. Offering our bodies as living sacrifices is our first act of worship. The Christian life, then, begins in worship. Ultimately, it will be consummated in worship. (More to come on that later!)

REGENERATION

Second, when we enter God's kingdom, we are regenerated. What does this mean?

When our first parents sinned, the human race was unplugged from the life of God. We became like toaster ovens without a current, all shiny and useful-looking, but with no real function or power. But when we are delivered from Satan's kingdom, we are "born again" or "born from above" by the power of the Spirit. Jesus told the Jewish

leader Nicodemus about this new or heavenly birth, and their conversation is recorded in John 3. Here are the major points Jesus made
in that exchange:

To begin with, the new birth is a necessity. Jesus did not tell
Nicodemus, "You *may* be born again" or "You *ought* to be born again."
No, He said, "You *must* be born again" (John 3:7, emphasis added).
Just as all of us have had a physical birth, so too all of us need a spiritual birth. Like leaving the womb, we leave one world (Satan's kingdom) to enter another (the kingdom of God). Then we are plugged
back into our power source as the Holy Spirit enters and works in us.
The lights go on. The darkness flees. Jesus is real. The Holy Spirit
enters and works in us. The Bible speaks to us. Prayer becomes an
adventure. The spiritual world comes alive and we are alive in it. We
sense God's hand upon us, leading us. We belong to God's people. We
have an eternal family and an eternal destiny. In order to live the lives
for which we were created, we must be born again.

Next, Jesus described the mystery of the new birth to Nicodemus: The Spirit is like the wind; it blows where it wills (John 3:8).
There is a play on words here: The Hebrew word for "spirit" is the
same as "wind." We don't know where the Spirit comes from or
where it goes, we can only see the effects. The Spirit's work is sovereign. When He makes us alive, it is a miracle of grace. God breaks
us out of Satan's grip, reconnects us to Himself, disrupts our sin
patterns and brings us His power and gifting for ministry. All of
this is God's miracle for us and in us.

Finally, Jesus told Nicodemus the basis for and starting place of
the new birth. This is crucial because He didn't describe some New
Age mystical experience or an altered state of consciousness. He
didn't talk about achieving nirvana.

To explain the source of the new birth, Jesus drew an analogy
between His future work on the cross and an episode recorded in the

Old Testament. After the children of Israel were delivered from Egypt, they rebelled against God. As a result, He sent a plague of deadly serpents and many people were bitten and died. Moses, the people's leader, cried out for mercy, and the Lord responded by commanding him to craft a serpent out of brass, put it on a pole and lift it up in the middle of the camp. He promised that all who looked to the serpent in faith would be healed (see Num. 21:4-9). For Jesus, this was a prophetic picture of what He would do for us on the cross. Like the serpent, He must be lifted up. When we look to the crucified Christ in faith, we are healed, but the healing and new birth *only* happen by a work of the Spirit. There, as our sins are forgiven, we are cleansed so that God through His Holy Spirit can enter into us.

Jesus concluded His conversation with Nicodemus by saying the most famous words in the Bible: "For God so loved the world that he gave his one and only Son, that whoever believes in him will not perish but have eternal life" (John 3:16). When we respond to this invitation, rather than perish, we have eternal life, starting now! Our spirits are made alive and plugged back into the living God, and the connection to the ultimate power Source changes our whole life: body, soul and spirit.

SANCTIFICATION

Hand in hand with submitting to Jesus' lordship and experiencing the new birth, when we enter God's kingdom we start to become more and more like Jesus Himself. This happens both by *crisis* and by *process*.

For many, conversion is a *crisis*. When I was a sophomore in high school, I heard Jim Rayburn (founder of Young Life) narrate the final hours of Jesus' life, graphically depicting His sufferings in a Mel Gibson sort of way. Jim said that there were two groups of people at the cross. First, there were those who mocked and cursed Jesus, who said, in effect, "Stay on the cross and stay out of my life."

Second, there was a much smaller group: Mary, Jesus' mother, and a few others who came, not to curse, but to pray. This group included a thief dying next to Jesus who begged him, "Remember me when you come into your kingdom" (Luke 23:42).

Then Jim said, "You are in one group or the other. You are either saying, 'Jesus, stay out of my life,' or you are kneeling at the cross praying, 'Jesus, remember me.' There is no fence to sit on because there is no fence." As I listened to Jim, I knew that I had never come to the cross to kneel and pray. I was part of the first group that said, "Jesus, stay on the cross and stay out of my life." But in that moment, I didn't want to be in that group any longer. When I understood that Jesus died the death that I deserved, I was broken and prayed, "Lord, remember me." I was born again. This crisis led to the *process* of getting to know God and myself over a lifetime. (Of course, there were a few more crises to come!)

In contrast to my experience, other people go through a *process* of conversion, much like a long labor to bring a child into the world. They may be raised as Christians, like my wife, Kathryn, but each (like Kathryn) must come to a place of personal surrender. This may not be dramatic or even conscious, but at some point, they know that they know Jesus and that is that.

No one can become a Christian apart from the work of God's Spirit. Paul's letter to the Romans tells us that if we do not have the Spirit of Christ, we do not belong to Him (see Rom. 8:9). During a crisis conversion, some experience the Spirit in radical ways. When my friend Mark McCoy—a young rock 'n' roll musician and heroin addict—accepted Jesus, he was filled with the Spirit, spoke in tongues *and* was healed of his addiction (without withdrawals) all in one dramatic night! But many other people are less conscious of the Spirit's manifested power and more conscious of the effects of His presence in their changing lives. Remember, He does not come to bear witness to Himself, but to Jesus (see John 15:26).

After either a crisis or process conversion, there is a *process* of becoming like Jesus. The Bible calls this "sanctification," which means to become holy just as Jesus is holy. While "holy" may not be a popular word, remember that it comes from the same root as "whole," which is a wonderful word indeed. What would it be like if all the sin and selfishness were sucked out of this world? It would be paradise! Sin screws us up. Jesus comes into our screwed-up humanity not only to cancel sin, but also to "unscrew us" and our world. He transforms us and makes us human again, fully like Himself. This transformation happens over a lifetime as we grow up into Him.

God also promises to fill us with His Spirit. Some call this being "empowered by the Spirit," and others, the "baptism of the Spirit." Many people actually feel and experience the Spirit coming over them to release His power and gifting in them. In the first century, this was expected. For many today, the experience may be subsequent to conversion, but it is all a part of what God has for us. In the words of Gordon Fee, to become a Christian is to become a "Spirit person."[2]

When the Spirit enters us, the *fruit* of the Spirit, such as love, joy and peace (see Gal. 5:22-23) begin to grow in us. This enables us to use the *gifts* of the Spirit, such as prophecy, healing and miracles (see 1 Cor. 12:7-11) for the good of others rather than for ourselves. We learn that *spiritual gifts are given to be given*. They are tools for ministry and service, to build up the Christian community and renew our common life. John Wimber used to say that when we move into ministry, we are like plumbers without a wrench. But at the moment we move to serve, God gifts us with the right tools to be effective. When we take the risk of faith, His Spirit gives us exactly what we need.

In sum, we are delivered from Satan's kingdom and born into God's kingdom by the Spirit through faith in Christ. But what's next? Surrender becomes our lifestyle. This is real worship, and it lies at the heart of Kingdom living.

CHAPTER 3

"HERE I AM TO WORSHIP"

If I had been told as a new Christian that the reason for my conversion was for me to become a worshiper, I would have been dumbfounded. As a dropout from a liberal mainline church, I had long been bored with liturgy, unsingable hymns and personality-driven sermons that offered little more than thin cheer.

Then Jesus met me, and I responded to Him. Suddenly, the lyrics of classic hymns began to make sense. When Christmas rolled around, I was amazed at how so many carols were infused with the gospel. I found an evangelical Presbyterian church with a preacher who made the Bible come alive. But worship? I never knew what it was. A few hymns punctuated by the Creed, prayers, readings and a choir anthem all seemed like the warm-up for the real deal: the sermon. It was not until many years later that I encountered satisfying corporate worship at the Anaheim Vineyard: 2,000 people singing *to* Jesus rather than *about* Jesus, using contemporary music and lyrics, pouring out their hearts, uninterrupted for half an hour. Tears streamed down most of the faces around me, and people were clearly in the presence of the Lord. I had never seen such engagement in worship before.

For some time now, I have participated in this revolution of worship. I have learned that the heart of biblical worship is surrender and that it begins at the moment of conversion. I have also learned that the aim of corporate worship is not simply to sing good theology or witness to our common experience of Christ. The object of our worship is God Himself, nothing less.[1] As we sing to Him rather than about Him, our focus is taken off of ourselves and directed to the throne, whether we are shouting high praise before God's awesomeness or kneeling in intimate devotion.

Jesus Himself set the outline for our worship in John 4:21-24. In His conversation with a Samaritan woman, Jesus said that worship no longer takes place in sacred *places* (such as the Jerusalem Temple), but in sacred *people*. He told the Samaritan woman that God is seeking worshipers who will worship Him in spirit and in truth. "In spirit" means that God initiates our worship. His Spirit enflames our spirits, and we turn to Him in praise and surrender. "In truth" means that worship must be centered on the truth, which is Jesus Himself (see John 14:6). As His Spirit stirs us to worship Him, we must repent of our idols and detach from addictions that power them. We must deny ourselves and worship Him in spirit and truth. This is for His glory and for our good.

Tom Wright wrote that we become like what (or who) we worship.[2] If we worship sex, we become lust-filled people. If we worship money, we become greedy people. If we worship people, we become co-dependent people. If we worship power, we become egotistical people.

> The idols of the nations are silver and gold,
> made by the hands of men.
> They have mouths, but cannot speak,
> eyes, but they cannot see;
> they have ears, but cannot hear,
> nor is there breath in their mouths.

Those who make them will be like them
and so will all who trust in them (Ps. 135:15-18).

Idols make us into themselves. But if we worship the living God, we become more and more like Him in our intentions and actions. We participate in His agenda to repopulate the planet with images of Himself. When we enter the kingdom of God, our destiny is to become like Jesus. God-centered—not self-centered—worship affects this transformation. So how do we worship the King? Let me begin by painting a picture for you.

Imagine you live in sixteenth-century England and you're being ushered into the presence of King Henry VIII. He is on his throne, which is placed high upon a golden platform, and he is dressed in rich, royal robes. He wears a jeweled crown and holds a scepter, the symbol of his reign. Surrounding him are his courtiers, servants, advisors, counselors and ambassadors from other countries. They, too, are royally dressed. The hall is magnificent, with high gothic arches holding vaulted ceilings. Armed guards stand at attention and ladies-in-waiting and other dignitaries line the walls. You enter through high doors and approach the throne, walking down a long red carpet. How do you come before such a king?

First, you address him properly. You call him, "Your Majesty." You recite how just, powerful and gracious he is and give him the honor due his office and his person. Second, you make your act of submission. You bow low before him (you might even prostrate yourself). Third, you give him gifts to win his favor, especially if you represent another nation or power. Fourth, you present your intercessions (your petitions), which could be as simple as "Your Majesty, we need a new well in our town" or as grave as a plea for clemency. Fifth, you wait for his answer, his provision, his judgment, his mercy. Finally, if the answer is positive, you leave rejoicing, bursting with excitement to tell all your friends about your good fortune.

This is the proper way to approach an earthly king, and it should be the pattern for our worship of the Eternal King. Not every element will be in every corporate worship experience, but we need to learn the pattern. The model is biblical, and following it will build us up to become the persons and community God has designed us to be.

GIVING THE KING HIS DUE

Just as with an earthly king, when we come before the King of kings, we bring high praise. Before all else, we open our hands and our hearts and give Him the honor and glory due Him. This standard is established for us in Psalm 100:

> Shout for joy to the Lord, all the earth.
> Worship the Lord with gladness;
> come before him with joyful songs.
> Know that the Lord is God.
> It is he who made us, and we are his . . .
> Enter his gates with thanksgiving
> and his courts with praise;
> give thanks to him and praise his name.
> For the Lord is good and his love endures forever;
> his faithfulness continues through all generations.

Notice how vocal and physical this is. We are in the King's presence. We are to shout—our joy cannot be contained! We are to sing to Him, not simply about Him. He is God. He is the Creator. He is good. His love endures forever. He is faithful through all generations.

So cheer up and go for it. Bellow it out (at least in private!) and put your whole self into worship. Get physical: "Lift up your hands in the sanctuary and praise the Lord" (Ps. 134:2). Sway to the beat: "Let them praise his name with dancing and make music to him with tambourine and harp. For the LORD delights in his people" (Ps. 149:3-4). You might even burst into some holy hilarity: "Our mouths were filled with laughter, our tongues with songs of joy" (Ps. 126:2).

This is not simply Old Testament stuff. Paul wrote this instruction to the Philippians: "Rejoice in the Lord always. I will say it again: Rejoice!" (4:4). He told the Ephesians, "Do not get drunk on wine, which leads to debauchery. Instead, be filled [keep on being filled] with the Spirit. Speak to one another with psalms, hymns and spiritual songs. Sing and make music in your heart to the Lord, always giving thanks to God the Father for everything in the name [authority] of our Lord Jesus Christ" (5:18-20). The author of the book of Hebrews paints this picture of worship:

> But you have come to Mount Zion, to the heavenly Jerusalem, the city of the living God. You have come to thousands upon thousands of angels in joyful assembly, to the church of the firstborn, whose names are written in heaven. You have come to God, the judge of all men [and women], to the spirits of righteous men made perfect, to Jesus the mediator of a new covenant . . . Therefore, since we are receiving a kingdom that cannot be shaken, let us be thankful, and so worship God acceptably with reverence and awe, for our "God is a consuming fire" (12:22-24,29).

In the book of Revelation, John has a vision of God's throne room. All creation joins the heavenly choir, as John reports: "Then

I heard every creature in heaven and on earth and under the earth and on the sea, and all that is in them singing: 'To him who sits on the throne and to the Lamb [Jesus] be praise and honor and glory and power for ever and ever!'" (5:13).

As John Wimber said, when we worship corporately, the whole congregation is the choir, singing before an Audience of One (God Himself). High praise will expand our vision of God. High praise will elevate our spirits. High praise alone is due to God for His majesty and His mighty name. We need to come into His presence and tell Him how great He is—to get the focus off ourselves and onto Him! When we offer Him high praise, He shows up.

BOWING BEFORE THE KING

After we bring our praise and adoration, it's time to make our act of submission. If we were coming before an earthly king, men would bow and women would curtsy. In ancient courts, this deference was a matter of life and death: bowing before the king was a literal acknowledgment that he held your life in his hands. Consider these Old Testament texts:

When the woman from Tekoa went to the king [David], she fell with her face to the ground to pay him honor (2 Sam. 14:4).

Joab fell with his face to the ground to pay him [David] honor, and he blessed the king (2 Sam. 14:22).

Then the king summoned Absalom, and he came in and bowed down with his face to the ground before the king. And the king kissed Absalom (2 Sam. 14:33).

In the same way, the King of heaven holds our lives in His hands, and our worship should express our surrender to Him: "Come, let us sing for joy to the Lord; let us shout aloud to the Rock of our salvation . . . For the Lord is the great God, the great King above all gods . . . Come, let us bow down in worship [literally "fall down"], let us kneel before the Lord our Maker; for he is our God" (Ps. 95:1-7).

The themes of surrender and submission run through the New Testament as well. Paul calls us to offer our bodies as living sacrifices to the Lord, and he identifies this sacrifice as our spiritual act of worship (see Rom. 12:1). John's vision of heaven's throne room ends with this: "The four living creatures [mighty angels] said, 'Amen,' and the elders fell down and worshiped" (Rev. 5:14). We live this new life with Jesus in continual surrender. We surrender to His Word, His Spirit, His voice, His present and His future for us. Paradoxically, our freedom is found in surrender. God created us to become perpetual worshipers. This worship begins the moment Jesus claims us and we give our hearts to Him.

GIFTS FOR THE KING

Once we make our act of submission, we bring our gifts. If we were coming before an earthly king, this would serve to honor him (although in ancient times, the gift might also be a bribe!). Even today, presidents and prime ministers bring gifts to each other on official visits.

This habit also has its parallel in our biblical worship to God. In the Old Testament, we find instructions to bring our tithes and offerings to the Lord: "Sacrifice thank offerings to God, fulfill your vows to the Most High" (Ps. 50:14). As we have already seen, in the New Testament, Paul exhorts us to offer our bodies as living sacrifices to the Lord. We no longer bring a bull or lamb as a blood offering—the

final blood sacrifice was made by Jesus on the cross—but we don't
come before the throne empty handed. We bring ourselves. We are the
sacrifice placed on the altar of worship. So we fall down in surrender
and rise up as our offering to the Lord. John Wimber once said that
commitment is time, energy and money. As we offer ourselves, we
offer these practical gifts as signs of our commitment to God.

In the New Testament, one of the major purposes for giving
money is providing for the poor. The apostles blessed Paul's ministry to the Gentiles and exhorted him to remember the poor. He
commented in his letter to the Galatian church that this was "the
very thing I was eager to do" (2:10). As a result, Paul spent consid-
erable time and energy collecting money for the impoverished
church in Jerusalem. Even poor Gentile churches such as those in
Macedonia (northern Greece) gave well beyond their means. Paul
wrote, "For I testify that they gave as much as they were able, and
even beyond their ability. Entirely on their own, they urgently
pleaded with us for the privilege of sharing in this service to the
saints" (2 Cor. 8:3-4).

God is not building an earthly Temple. He is building a spiritual Temple, made of people who are living stones, cemented to
each other with the keystone (Christ) above all (see Eph. 2:19-22).
Having said this, it is proper for local churches to use some
resources to house the community and pay a professional staff,
but we need to keep our values straight. All gifts given to us by
God are to be given away, especially to those unable to care for
themselves. The gospel is exploding in impoverished developing
nations. As a nation and as a Church, we need to give gifts to our
King by supporting debt remission and investing in material and
medical assistance for these destitute nations. In this, we will learn
what Jesus meant when He said, "It is more blessed to give than to
receive" (Acts 20:35).

PETITIONING THE KING

Having given our gifts to the King, we now bring Him our petitions and intercessions. In sixteenth-century England, Henry VIII had both the power and the authority to meet the needs of his realm. In our modern democracies in which politicians jockey for votes, this may be hard for us to understand. Yet God has authority and power over *all things* and is ready and anxious to answer our prayers. He invites us to have a conversation with Him just the same way we would talk to a trusted friend.

Our first petition is for forgiveness. As the 12 Steps of Alcoholics Anonymous teaches us, we each need to take a moral inventory of ourselves. Who have we hurt or wronged? Who do we need to forgive for wronging us? We ask our sovereign King, who is also our loving Father, to lift our burden. As we lay out our transgressions, God is faithful and just to cleanse us from all unrighteousness (see 1 John 1:9). At the center of the Kingdom is the cross. Satan seeks to imprison us in shame and guilt, but we take every sinful thought and every rotten response to the foot of the cross and leave it there. Listen to David:

> Blessed is he
> whose transgressions are forgiven,
> whose sins are covered.
> Blessed is the man
> whose sin the Lord does not count against him . . .
> When I kept silent,
> my bones wasted away
> through my groaning all day long . . .
> Then I acknowledged my sin to you
> and did not cover up my iniquity.
> I said, "I will confess

my transgressions to the LORD"—
and you forgave
the guilt of my sin (Ps. 32:1-5).

We are to confess our sins both to God and to each other, for if
we remain silent, our sins keep a grip on us, growing like mold. As
James promises, "The prayer offered in faith will make the sick person
well; the Lord will raise him up. If he has sinned, he will be forgiven.
Therefore confess your sins to each other and pray for each other so
that you may be healed" (5:15-16). Confession not only clears the
lines with the Lord, it also heals us—spiritually, emotionally and even
physically. Moreover, as we forgive others, we release them from the
prison of our unforgiveness. Resentment no longer controls our lives
by feeding our pain and anger over what has been done to us.

So, we keep short accounts, take a moral inventory, make confession a daily discipline and bring every sin to the gracious King.
Next, we ask God to meet our needs and the needs of others. Listen
to David:

Give ear to my words, O LORD,
consider my sighing.
Listen to my cry for help,
my King and my God,
for to you I pray.
In the morning, O LORD, You hear my voice;
in the morning I lay my requests before you
and wait in expectation (Ps. 5:1-3).

David not only brought his needs to the Lord, but he also expected an answer. Again, in the New Testament, Paul exhorts us, "Do not
be anxious about anything, but in everything, by prayer and petition,

with thanksgiving, present your requests to God. And the peace of God, which transcends all understanding, will guard your hearts and your minds in Christ Jesus" (Phil. 4:6-7). He asked the Ephesians for personal prayer and fully expected supernatural answers: "Pray also for me, that whenever I open my mouth, words may be given me so that I will fearlessly make known the mystery of the gospel, for which I am an ambassador in chains. Pray that I may declare it fearlessly, as I should" (6:19-20).

WAITING ON THE KING

Once we've brought our requests to the King, we must wait for His answer. As with an earthly monarch, the response may come in a moment or after some time has lapsed. It may be exactly what we want, or it may be what He wants and believes is best for us. Remember, God is sovereign, and we aren't.

Here is an amazing thing about our God: He answers prayer and speaks to us during times of worship. He is not like the deaf and dumb idols. We can hear His voice as we open our spirits to Him, but for this to happen we need to learn to sit in silence before Him. We need to pay special attention to any spontaneous thoughts or Scripture verses that may cross our mind. And we need discernment. We need to ask ourselves, *Is this simply my voice, my wishful thinking? Is this the voice of the enemy? Or is this the voice of God?*

God's people expected Him to speak. David wrote, "I sought the LORD, and he answered me; he delivered me from all my fears" (Ps. 34:4). But does this really happen? In Psalm 4:1, David writes, "Answer me when I call to you, O my righteous God. Give me relief from my distress; be merciful and hear my prayer." In the very next verse God responds, "How long, O men, will you turn my glory into shame? How long will you love delusions and seek false gods?" (v. 2). God gets to the heart of the issue: David's distress came from idolatry, and this block had to be removed. In essence the Lord was saying, "Put down the idols and become godly. Then I will act."

Martin Buber remarked that biblical faith is dialogical.[3] God speaks, we answer; we speak, God answers. But if we aren't listening, we will never hear. It is as if when the phone rings, we pick it up, blab and then quickly hang up, wondering why the person on the other end never said anything. When we stand before the King, we must listen for His voice. He will answer in His time and in His ways.

Throughout the Old and New Testaments, God's voice is often heard through the gift of prophecy. Again and again, Israel's rulers consulted prophets to receive rebuke, comfort and direction. Yet what was limited in the Old Testament to a specially called few is now poured out upon all of us (see Acts 2:17). We are to eagerly desire the gift of prophecy, hearing the word of the Lord and speaking it to others. This word is current, uplifting, comforting and, at times, predictive. God is speaking. Are we listening? We need to worship with the expectation that we will hear personally from Him. Remember, in responding to the gospel, we already have.

We also come to the great King whose rule is one of justice and righteousness. Although He is patient and longsuffering, He judges injustice and unrighteousness. So, as we pray to Him, we ask for His justice to be done. "Awake, my God, decree justice. Let the assembled peoples gather around you. Rule over them from on high; let the LORD judge the peoples. Judge me, O LORD" (Ps. 7:6-8). As we pray these prayers, our consciences will be sharpened and our moral fiber strengthened. We will share God's passion for the lonely, the lost, the widow, the orphan, the addicted, the malnourished, the poor, the illiterate, the sick, the aged, the stranger and the alien in our midst. We will also share His passion for alleviating their suffering.

REJOICING IN THE KING

As the fulfillment of our praise, submission, gifts, petitions and waiting on the Lord, God grants us His presence. In the Old Testament, a sign of God's favor was His face turned toward His people. David wrote, "He observes the sons of men; his eyes examine them. The LORD examines the righteous . . . For the Lord is righteous, he loves justice; upright men [and women] see his face" (Ps. 11:4-7).

This longing to see and know the King face to face was marvelously fulfilled in the New Testament when God stepped decisively into our history through His Son Jesus. As we have seen, He also steps into our hearts: The Lord Jesus Christ becomes personal and intimate with us when we receive Him. He is both exalted in heaven and in our hearts through His Spirit.

We exit our audience with the King, praising His name and witnessing His grace and goodness to those still held captive in the counterfeit kingdom of darkness. As we depart, it is as if the King steps down from His throne and walks with us out into the parking lot, down the street, into our homes, off to school, to the day-care center, into the business world, into our families, into our marriages, into our friendships, into our gardens, into our play time and into all the battles of life. Jesus' promises are clear: He will never leave us nor forsake us (see Heb. 13:5). No one can pluck us out of His hand (see John 10:28). He is with us always, even to the close of the age (see Matt. 28:20). "[Nothing] will be able to separate us from the love of God in Christ Jesus our Lord" (Rom. 8:39).

As we have already mentioned, not every element in this structure will appear in every corporate worship service. At times, we may simply center on high praise; at others, we may center on repentance and intimacy. But over time, healthy worship will embrace all aspects of this design. And while we can learn much from the worship structure I've described in this chapter, we must remember that when the Spirit comes with power and gifts, spontaneity often follows (see 1 Cor. 14). As God moves in our midst, there is no contradiction between order and freedom in worship. We learn both to plan well and to become sensitive to Him in the moment.

We have a King, exalted in holiness, faithful in friendship, who is also our loving Father. This makes His rule all the more wonderful. As we enter into worship, we enter into a life of discipleship. We become Christ followers. We become apprentices of Jesus.[4] We ask Him to be our sponsor so that we may become like Him and learn how to live.[5] It's to this that we now turn.

CHAPTER 4

LIFE IN THE KINGDOM: COME ON IN!

Why do people come to Christ and not mature in their faith? Why are there so many nominal Christians? Why doesn't the Church have a greater impact on society? Why? Why? Why?

The answer is that we have a thin understanding of the gospel and the Christian life. Salvation becomes either a past event ("I got saved") or a future hope ("One day I will to go to heaven"). But, as we have seen, salvation at its core is our transfer from the kingdom of Satan into the kingdom of God. There, we live a grace-based life together in the power of the Spirit. Jesus' bold and unflinching call, "Follow Me," releases us from our old lives as He unequivocally attaches us to Himself. In following Him, we become like Him. We extend His ministry, planting cells (churches) of Kingdom people who live out His Kingdom life. In responding to His call, we also embrace His agenda: "Come . . . and I will make you fishers of men [and women]" (Mark 1:17). To belong to Jesus is to follow Jesus. As we grow closer to His heart, we draw closer to what's *on* His heart: people.

Let's see how God inaugurates our life into the Kingdom.

THE SETTING

First-century Jews were obsessed by their Messianic hope. Their land was occupied by Rome, and they cried out for deliverance, the final exodus that would usher in the promised kingdom of God. The harder the Romans pushed, the harder the Jews pushed back. Messianic pretenders came and went as Rome crushed every hint of revolt. The Roman Empire fully intended to keep its grip on Palestine—the land wedge between Europe, Asia and Africa—and the Romans' tenacity only made the Jews more furious and more fanatical.

So when the news got out about the new prophet in Galilee who was performing miracles and announcing the coming Kingdom, expectations soared. Many believed that he could be the one, and that this could be the moment. They wondered if God at last had intervened to expel the infidels and restore the fortunes of His people.

The Jewish hope was that God Himself would intervene—that just as He rescued His people from Egypt through Moses, so He would rescue His people from Rome through the Messiah. A new King from the line of David, the heir to the throne of Israel, would establish His kingdom, slaughter the occupying army, tear down the pagan shrines, gather the Jews from their dispersion, cleanse the land and rebuild Jerusalem. God Himself would come to reign, glorifying His Temple and welcoming any Gentiles who sought to live according to His Law. The land would flourish with peace and prosperity. Many first-century Jews even added to this vision of God's coming the final judgment, the resurrection of the dead, and Eden restored in the new heaven and Earth.[1] When John the Baptist appeared on the scene, these hopes were the backdrop to his fiery preaching.

Rabbinical teaching of the day said that if all Israel would repent for just one day, Messiah—the anointed King—would come. Following that tradition, John called people to turn from sin and back to God. People trekked from all over Israel to the Jordan River to confess their sins and receive John's baptism as a sign of cleansing. In a symbolic way, he excommunicated unrepentant Jews and then baptized them back into God's covenant, much like what was done to Gentile converts.[2]

In the midst of his preaching and baptizing, John suddenly one day saw Jesus standing on the riverbank. As Jesus presented Himself for baptism, John protested, "I need to be baptized by you" (Matt. 3:14). How could the sinless One submit to a baptism for sinners? But Jesus commanded John to baptize Him. What was going on here?

The common Jewish belief was that when Messiah came, the jig was up: Fire would fall from heaven to consume all God's enemies. With this belief on his mind, John was ready to abandon his role and have Jesus take over. After all, John was a sinner just like everyone else! Only Jesus, as the Anointed One, had the legal and moral right to execute divine justice.

But Jesus refused. His mission was not to bring God's judgment down on people; His mission was to break Satan's back and lift God's judgment from them. He came not to condemn the world, but that the world may be saved through Him (see John 3:17). So Jesus stood on the riverbank with the pimps and prostitutes, the hucksters and hustlers. He was, as Dietrich Bonhoeffer stated, "the man for others."[3] Even more, He was the God for others.

Cheer up! The sinless Son of God, the Messianic King, stands with us, not against us. He stands with us amid our demons, our diseases and our unbelief, even when our taunts are directed against Him. He stands with us in our pride, our jealousy, our sexual seductions, our violence, our religious exploitations, our racism, our hypocrisy and our guilt and shame. He stands with us as we peer into the hole in the soul, the ache deep within each of us.

His baptism in water anticipated His baptism in blood when He hung on a cross as the Lamb of God who took away the sins of the world (see John 1:29).

If we are to follow Jesus, we must join Him on the riverbank. It is here that the Kingdom is first revealed, because it is here that the King is first revealed. To join Jesus means that we acknowledge our own sin, repent and surrender to Him. We have no right to stand with John and denounce sinners: We come to the Jordan with broken hearts and come to have our hearts broken. This is our entry point into the Kingdom.

THE EVENT

When John baptized Jesus, it was as if all of Israel's history was summed up in that one symbolic act. Just as Israel went through the Red Sea in the first Exodus, so Jesus went through the Jordan in the final exodus. Instead of deliverance from Pharaoh, however, Jesus offered deliverance from Satan himself, transferring all who follow Him into the kingdom of God.[4]

To become a Christian is to become a "Christ follower," to die to the old life and rise into a new life in Him, cleansed and reborn. The sign of this death and resurrection is our baptism, and Jesus Himself is our model.

The Church calls baptism a "sacrament," an outward sign of inward grace. Baptism is the rite of entry into the Christian life. It not only symbolizes cleansing of sin (water) but also the death of our old lives (as we go down into the water) and resurrection to our new lives in Christ (as we rise up from the water; see Rom. 6:3-4). Baptism signifies our spiritual exodus, our deliverance from Satan's kingdom and our entry into God's kingdom. But baptism is not just a symbol; it is also an event. God meets us in a special way in our baptism, just as He met Jesus in His.

My friend Bill Greig II once asked me to meet his Muslim friend Parvis, who had fled from Iran with his wife and small son. After arriving in the United States, Parvis became depressed and suicidal. But one night, he had a dream in which Jesus came to him and washed him in a fountain. (Parvis knew nothing of Jesus at that time, but he somehow knew it was Him.) Parvis began to weep in his sleep, and the next day his depression was gone. Later, while driving a cab in Denver, he picked up Bill Greig and shared this dream with him. Bill responded by telling Parvis about Jesus Christ and sending him a Bible.

Three years later, Parvis and I stood on a beach in San Diego with a few other Christians. I asked him, "Do you renounce Islam as a false religion?" Parvis echoed, "I renounce Islam as a false religion." Then I asked, "Do you renounce Mohammed as a false prophet?" He echoed, "I renounce Mohammed as a false prophet." Then I asked, "Do you confess Jesus as your only Lord and Savior?" He affirmed his confession. Then we walked into the Pacific, where Parvis was baptized. Parvis came out of the water a changed man. His baptism climaxed and sealed his conversion. Now, his passion is to take Jesus to the children of Iran.

THE DESCENT

When Jesus came up out of the Jordan River, an amazing thing happened: The skies ripped open and the Holy Spirit descended upon Him like a dove (see Mark 1:10). Heaven was no longer closed in judgment! God's connection with Earth is remade for us as the anointing of the Spirit of God comes upon the Son of God.

The Hebrew Scriptures promised that in the Age of Salvation, the Spirit would fall from heaven, bringing the prophetic word of God, raising the dead bones of Israel and breathing life into them again. The Spirit, once the gift of the favored few, would now be the permanent possession of all God's people.[5]

Specifically, the Spirit fell on Jesus, anointing Him for His Messianic ministry. When King David, Jesus' prototype, was called to become Israel's next ruler, the prophet Samuel anointed him with oil, and the Spirit fell on him (see 1 Sam. 16:13). Now, a greater David was here, anointed not by a prophet but by the Spirit Himself. By the power of the Spirit, Jesus would fulfill His Kingdom ministry. By the power of the Spirit, He would deliver us from Satan's dark rule, offering His body and blood as the final sacrifice for sin. By the power of the Spirit, He would conquer death and rise again into an indestructible life.

As the Second Person of the Triune God, the fully human and fully divine Jesus had always been in communion with the Holy Spirit. He was conceived by the Spirit in the Virgin Mary's womb, but now, at His baptism, He was filled and flooded with the Spirit's power. He had always known the *presence* of the Spirit, but now He experienced the *power* of the Spirit. This was the infallible sign that the Kingdom Age—the Age of Salvation—had dawned.

Just as we follow Christ into the waters of baptism to signify the death of our old lives and our resurrection to the new, we also must follow His baptism in the Spirit. As Jesus was anointed and empowered for His ministry, so we need to be anointed and empowered for our ministries. What happened to Him must happen to us. As we have seen, we cannot be born again apart from the presence of the Spirit. But, like Jesus, we need not only the Spirit's presence, but also His power. We need to be anointed with power from on high. If Jesus, God's eternal Son, needed the power of the Spirit for ministry, how is it that we think we can do with less?

This power is sorely lacking in so much of modern Christianity. The great preacher A. W. Tozer once said that if the Holy Spirit were taken from most churches, nothing would change. He added that we should not think of the Holy Spirit *and* power, but of the Holy Spirit *as* power.[6] God is restoring the power of the Spirit to His Church today. We too must join Jesus in the water to see the heavens open and the Spirit descend to empower us to do what Jesus does.

Have you been empowered by the Spirit? Listen to the words of Jesus:

> So I say to you: Ask [present imperative: "keep asking"] and it will be given to you; seek ["keep seeking"] and you will find; knock ["keep knocking"] and the door will be opened to you. For everyone who asks receives; he who seeks finds; and to him who knocks, the door will be opened. Which of you fathers, if your son asks for a fish, will give him a snake instead? Or if he asks for an egg, will give him a scorpion? If you, then, though you are evil, know how to give good gifts to your children, how much more will your Father in heaven give the Holy Spirit to those who ask him! (Luke 11:9-13).

If you have not yet been filled by the power of God's Spirit, ask Him to come now and fill you by praying this simple prayer: "Come, Holy Spirit, in Jesus' name. Fill me with Your life and power. Anoint me, like Jesus, for the Kingdom ministry You are calling me to do. I yield and wait expectantly for you. Amen."

THE AFFIRMATION

As Jesus stood dripping in the Jordan, the Father spoke. He had two confirmations for Jesus and for us in Him. The first was, "You are my Son, whom I love" (Mark 1:11). This is a reference to Psalm 2, in which God promised to place His Son, the anointed King, on Mount

Zion. From there, He would rule the nations. So, in announcing these words from Heaven, the Father affirmed that Jesus was called to be the final anointed King—the final David—who would usher in the Kingdom and establish the righteous rule of God throughout the nations.

This call to ministry, however, was also a confirmation of the Father's eternal relationship with His Son. Notice the present tense verbs: "You *are* my Son, whom I *love*." Behind this call to Messiahship, then, is Jesus' eternal Sonship with the Father. He was and is the Father's Son. They share the same nature and are held in a pure, eternal love relationship. The Father always loves the Son. He loves Him for who He is, not for what He does. He loves the Son in the depths of His being, freely and fully. All that Jesus does and endures is held in the Father's love.

When we begin our relationship with Jesus, we are adopted into God's family. We become sons and daughters of the King. Thus the Father's affirmation of His love for Jesus is also an affirmation of His love for us in His Son. He speaks over us, "You are my son, you are my daughter, whom I love." This is sheer grace, total acceptance, absolute and unchanging love from the depths of God's heart. The eternal love He has for His Son, He shares with us. Nothing can interrupt, compromise or separate us from this love.

It is so hard for us to believe that God loves us unconditionally because our lives are shot through with conditional love. From an early age, we are taught that performance brings acceptance. Our family systems, athletic systems, educational systems and social systems all teach the exact opposite of unconditional love. We are socialized by the message, "I love you, but . . ." ("I love you, but clean up your room"; "I love you, but get good grades"; "I love you, but go into Daddy's business"). It is a message most of us have heard our entire lives and still feel deep inside. Yet, as Rich Buhler says, if we confuse love with approval, we will spend our lives looking for approval when what we really need is love, pure and freely given.[7] God says, "I love you. Period." Here alone is free acceptance, the rock on which we can build our lives. Here alone is mental, emotional and physical health, which comes from the Father's heart. We can rest in the knowledge that He loves us every bit as much as He loves His Son. We enter the Kingdom through the gate marked, "I love you. Period."

After the Father confirmed His love for the Son, He gave Jesus His approval: "With you I am well pleased" (Mark 1:11). This is a reference to Isaiah 42, the first of a series of prophecies that climax in Isaiah 53, where the servant of the Lord sacrifices himself for the sins of the world. Jesus was to be the Davidic Warrior-King but also the Suffering Servant. As the Father speaks these words of confirmation to Christ, He commissions the Son not only to overturn Satan's kingdom but also to become the Lamb of God who takes away the sins of the world.

Thus, the Father here declared His unconditional love and approval for the Son. He approved of Jesus standing with us sinners on the riverbank. He approved of Jesus identifying with our sins in John's baptism. He was happy with the Son and the mission He embraced. He was tickled with Him, overjoyed with Him, filled with laughter and holy hilarity with Him. Indeed, He was well pleased.

In the same way, the Father loves us unconditionally and approves of us. After all, He is our creator as well as our redeemer, and He doesn't make junk! He approves of our genes, our personalities, our body image, our bone structures. He is pleased and tickled with us.

Can you hear this? The Father fully approves of you in His Son. He smiles on you, He winks at you, He embraces you. He even kisses you. You are special. You are approved. Even if you have been in the far country of disobedience and ruin, you have come home to the Father's heart. He rushes out to greet you, restores you fully to the family and throws a party for you. "Welcome home! I love you and I approve of you" (see Luke 15:20-24).

Again, it is so hard for us to hear and accept this because our world is filled with disapproval. We may have suffered criticism and judgment in our families. Many of us have been manipulated by our consumer society into believing that we are inadequate, sick, overweight, ugly, anxious and unhappy—all so that it can market more products to us. Moreover, we may even have had disapproval heaped upon us in a judgmental, self-righteous church.

Yet all of this pales in comparison to the disapproval we heap on ourselves. We are our own worst enemies. But Jesus has come for us, and in Him we are loved and approved of by the Father. He is well pleased with us! Now, with this unbelievable affirmation, we can begin to truly live our new lives. We can believe what the Father says to us in His Son. With this radical change in self-concept, our emotions, fantasies and behaviors will begin to change accordingly. Indeed, we will truly be born again.

BREAKTHROUGH/BATTLE PATTERN

Immediately after Jesus was baptized by John, the Spirit led Him into the wilderness. Remember, as the Messiah, Jesus reenacts Israel's history in Himself. Thus, just as Israel was led into the wilderness for 40 years in the first Exodus, Jesus would be led into the wilderness for 40 days in the final exodus. Just as Israel was tempted in the wilderness, Jesus would also be tempted in the wilderness. But now the temptation was not simply to rebel and return to Egypt. Satan himself would design the trio of temptations to sidetrack Jesus from His Messianic destiny (see Matt. 4:1-11).

Satan's first temptation was for Christ to be a materialistic Messiah, to turn stones into bread to meet His own and others' physical needs. The second temptation was for Him to be a spectacular Messiah, to throw Himself off the pinnacle of the Temple and wow the crowd. The third temptation was for Him to be a political Messiah, to claim the kingdoms of the world by worshiping their overlord, the devil himself. But Jesus fought back. At each turn, He exposed the devil's lies with the Word of God. Having rejected these false alternatives, Jesus was now ready to enter His ministry. He would be the Davidic Warrior-King, overcoming the kingdom of Satan. And He would be the Suffering Servant of the Lord, bearing away our sins in His bloody death.

What we learn from this progression is the Breakthrough/Battle pattern. After the breakthrough of Jesus' baptism with the power of the Spirit and the confirmation of the Father's approval, He had to go into the wilderness to battle Satan's seductive alternatives to God's power and love. We will experience this same pattern at work in our own life as we follow Jesus: The enemy will tempt us to build our life around our physical needs and passions, wow people through the magic of our power or personality, and manipulate others by "owning" the kingdoms of this world.

Be ready! Satan will attack you, tempt you and try to seduce you at your weakest points. Peter warns, "Be self-controlled and alert. Your enemy the devil prowls around like a roaring lion looking for someone to devour. Resist him, standing firm in the faith, because you know that your brothers [and sisters] throughout the world are undergoing the same kind of suffering" (1 Pet. 5:8-9).

Yet we are not alone. We are in this battle together with all of God's people in every generation. Jesus goes before us in this war. The devil is a defeated enemy. Through Jesus, together we will triumph as His people.

FOLLOWING CHRIST

Belonging to Jesus means attaching ourselves exclusively to Him. This is real faith and is accomplished by His grace alone. But to belong to Jesus also means to embrace His agenda. He is going fishing for people and wants to take us with Him as agents and instruments of His kingdom. We are out to ransack the kingdom of Satan and extend the kingdom of God. Everything the Father has for the Son is ours as joint-heirs with Christ. We are seated with Him in heavenly places, and when He returns, we will be glorified with Him.[8]

So, we enter the Kingdom by repentance and faith to become true worshipers. As we go through our exodus—our baptism, dying to our old lives to live new lives—we are not only reborn but also empowered for Kingdom ministry. We are baptized in water and in the power of the Spirit. The Father anoints us with His Spirit and says to us through the Son, "I love you and I am happy with you!" In Jesus, we are called to battle against the darkness and lay down our lives for the least and the lost. This is life in the Kingdom. This is life as God created and redeemed it to be.

CHAPTER 5

PROCLAIM THE KINGDOM

It is often said that the Church either preaches bad news or offers good advice. Neither of these are the gospel. Although people may feel convicted or counseled by what is said, their hearts and their history remain unchanged.

For many, preaching has lost its value. People say, "Don't preach to me" or "Your voice is preachy." They view preaching as a harangue that pummels people with negatives. Preachers, people think, often have an artificial voice and irritating mannerisms. They pronounce "God" as "Gawd." They either read their sermon in a monotone or prance and pace, entertaining the crowd.

For many successful megachurches today, preaching consists of little more than cheap, pop-psychological advice giving. Rarely is the word "sin" ever mentioned. The preacher's continual smile radiates success and draws crowds to his self-help messages that are disguised with selected Scriptures. For post-moderns, the pastor may sit on a stool or couch, show video clips and "share" in an effort to avoid the appearance of preaching at all costs. The intensity of the Kingdom's authority is gone.

I was once invited to address a pastors' retreat, and I asked my psychiatrist friend, David Sunday, what he would say to these pastors. He replied, "Most congregations today are out to kill you. The less the people in the congregation do, the more the pastor exhorts them, 'You have to tithe,' 'You need to be committed,' 'Get involved,' 'Come to church.' But the members in the congregation hate these legalisms, and they soon become passive-aggressive. The more the pastor demands, the angrier they become. They give less and less and move to the back of the sanctuary where they sit grim-faced. The less they do, the more the preacher has to do. Finally, the pastor bails, or it kills him." This is the sorry state of many congregations in which preaching has become a negative exercise with negative results.

Contrary to much of our church experience, Jesus comes with the Word of God, a divine message that is true, arresting and riveting. But what is this good news? What does it consist of?

THE KINGDOM OF GOD

Mark 1:14-15 states, "After John was put in prison, Jesus went into Galilee, proclaiming the good news of God. 'The time has come [is fulfilled],' he said. 'The kingdom of God is near [at hand, within reach]. Repent and believe the good news." Jesus brings the good news. It is not bad news (like so much traditional evangelism), nor is it merely good advice or a psychological "quick-fix." It is the message of God's gladness. Because it is God's good news, it must be spoken, shared and proclaimed—even from the rooftops.

So, first, Jesus' good news has to do with the fullness of time. The *New International Version* gives us a weak translation of Jesus' words in Mark 1:15, "The time has come." The original Greek conveys the meaning that the time is fulfilled. Contrary to the end times doom and gloom preaching that we often hear, time has not run out but has filled up to overflowing. This is the hour that Israel longs for. This is the hour the Gentiles search for. This is the moment, this is the crisis, and nothing will ever be the same again. Time has reached its fullness.

Second, Jesus' good news is all about the Kingdom: "The kingdom of God is near." Again, the *New International Version* provides a possible translation of the original Greek, but it is weak. The basic meaning of the verb used here is not temporal—that is, "The kingdom of God is close," in the way that lunchtime might be close at the end of the morning. Instead, the meaning is spatial, as in "The kingdom of God is at hand," much like this book is at hand or within reach. So the real meaning is that the King (Messiah) has come, and if we reach out and touch Him, we will touch the Kingdom. Likewise, as He touches us, we are also touched by the Kingdom, the rule and reign of God.

What then does "kingdom of God" mean? To talk about the kingdom of God is to talk about the *kingship* of God. It is dynamic, all-embracing and on the move. God is the King and He has His palace and His throne room in heaven. He has His retainers, the angelic hosts. He has His subjects, the angels, humans and all other forms of life. He has His realm, the heavens and the earth. In His love, He gives us the freedom to choose for or against Him. In His justice, He judges us accordingly. Although we have chosen to revolt, He comes after us to rescue us, forgive us and restore us to Himself. One day, His perfect reign will be manifest throughout His transformed creation. On that day, the redeemed will worship and serve Him out of cleansed and glad hearts. For now, His rule—His kingdom—has broken in on us and is advancing throughout the earth.

The presence of the Kingdom is good news because it means that God's presence has returned and that Satan's kingdom is under siege. Sins are forgiven, the sick are healed, the demonized are delivered, the exiles come home, and the age to come is upon us. But what does "the age to come" mean?

THE AGE TO COME

The Jews distinguished between two ages: this present evil age and
the age of salvation to come. With the arrival of Jesus into this world,
the age to come broke into this age, and we now live at its intersection. Our future hope has, in part, been realized: The kingdom of
God is here, but it is not fully here. Our world is still fallen, but it is
being redeemed. We live between the "already" and the "not yet."[1]

Thus, rather than waiting for the end to come, we are already living in the end times that will be consummated when Jesus returns.
His death guarantees our acquittal on the Day of Judgment, and His
resurrection guarantees our resurrection from the dead. The transformation of this decaying world began with the event of His resurrection. Let me illustrate what this means.

I boarded a British Airways flight from Los Angeles to London.
As I sat down, a stewardess offered me a plaid blanket made of
Scottish wool. Next, she poured me a cup of English breakfast tea
with milk. As I relaxed, the TV monitor began to play regal music and
show scenes of London. I was mesmerized. There was Buckingham
Palace, the Tower of London, St. Paul's Cathedral, Harrods, and the
bridges over the Thames. Here I was in Los Angeles, but I was already
tasting England, thanks to my blanket, tea and video. Likewise,
although we are still in this fallen world, we are already tasting the
Kingdom. We are born again. We are worshiping the King. We are
being filled with the Spirit. And, as we shall see, we are sharing in
Jesus' Kingdom ministry.

But we still await the consummation of the Kingdom with
Jesus' return—the "not yet" that is still to come. Jesus preaches in
the indicative; He announces what God is doing. This is the Word
of God, the overwhelming and triumphant good news. Jesus never
qualifies His proclamation of the good news with "I hope the

Kingdom is here" or "Perhaps the Kingdom is here." Neither does He propose a dialogue as to whether the kingdom of God is present in this world or not. He simply declares it with His authority. He stands with all the prophets before Him and states, "Thus says the Lord . . ."

But Jesus didn't just come to tell us the good news regarding the Kingdom. In true Kingdom preaching, the imperative always follows the indicative. So Jesus also told people what they must do to receive the Kingdom: "Repent and believe the good news." To "repent" implies a change in course. We have gone away from God, so now we must reverse course and turn toward Him. Repentance also involves surrender and sorrow for our sins. But there is more. As N. T. Wright shows, to "repent" means to surrender one's agenda for Jesus' agenda.[2] It means to take on His Kingdom message and ministry.

This is clearly sketched out for us by Luke. When Jesus went into the synagogue at Nazareth, He was handed the Isaiah scroll and read the following words from Isaiah 61:

The Spirit of the Lord is on [upon] me, because he has anointed me to preach good news to the poor. He has sent me to proclaim freedom for the prisoners [captives] and recovery of sight for the blind, to release the oppressed, to proclaim the year of the Lord's favor (Luke 4:18-19).

Jesus then sat down to teach and deliver His thesis: "Today this scripture is fulfilled in your hearing" (Luke 4:21) or, as we might say, "In your face!" The remainder of Luke's Gospel then becomes a commentary on this text: As Isaiah promised, Jesus evangelized the poor, released those captive to demons, healed the blind and the sick and liberated the oppressed. He proclaimed to the people that this was the year of the Lord's favor and that God's kingdom was breaking in on them. When John the Baptist's disciples inquire as to whether Jesus was the Messiah, he answers, "Go back and report to John what you have seen and heard: The blind receive sight, the lame walk, those who have leprosy are cured, the deaf hear, the dead are raised, and the good news is preached to the poor" (Luke 7:22). What Isaiah promised, Jesus fulfilled.

So when we believe the indicative that the Kingdom is within reach, we must repent by adopting Jesus' agenda for ministry as our own. In other words, we must become Christ followers. Next, we must believe the good news. We then enter the Kingdom through the gate marked "Good News."

TAKING AN ACTIVE ROLE

When it comes to sharing the good news, most churches have plenty of the indicative, especially Bible-teaching churches. Many see the imperative aspect of sharing the good news as a call for conversion or as a list of oughts and shoulds given to the congregation that tends to put them back under the law. Unfortunately, most churches have no structured way for people to respond to the indicative or the imperative. The sermon ends with a prayer, a hymn and the benediction. But where do people go from there? To the patio for coffee. But what about Jesus' agenda? Where are the blind healed? When do the lame walk? Where are lepers cured? When do the deaf hear? And what about evangelizing the poor?

The need to take an active role in the good news became apparent to me when I met John Wimber in 1983. During a time of deep personal pain in my life, a friend encouraged me to attend the Anaheim Vineyard. I did so, not knowing what to expect. The worship service at the church overwhelmed me. John's informal teaching style and solid biblical content lowered my defenses. Then he moved into hands-on ministry. He gave a flurry of prophetic words about certain individuals' physical and emotional pain that he believed God wanted to heal or minister to that night. Then as scores of people responded, John directed them to teams of people who were equipped to pray for them. Many were either healed or their condition significantly improved.

Coming from a straight evangelical background, this was all new to me. But as I watched John and his teams, I learned that we too in the Church could do all of the things that Jesus did. It was not merely an issue of learning theology, knowing biblical content, embracing high ethical standards, resolving relational conflicts or even growing in spiritual disciplines. It was more about fulfilling Jesus' agenda for ministry in the here and now, in time and space, in our world.

Kingdom preaching must include Kingdom ministry. The indicative must be joined to the imperative. As John Wimber once taught, "Jesus is the Word/Worker, and everybody gets to play." If we are to follow Jesus' agenda for ministry, we too must become Word/Workers ourselves.

Are you open to this? Would you like to evangelize the poor, heal the sick and cast out demons? Would you like to participate in delivering this fallen creation from Satan's grasp? Would you like to be a real Christ follower? You can't settle for less!

CHAPTER 6

CALL TO KINGDOM MINISTRY

What does it mean to live as a Christian? What does it mean to be a Christ follower, an apprentice of Jesus? What does it mean to get beyond "sin management"?[1] How does Jesus Himself define our new life? It all begins and ends with discipleship.

Jesus began His ministry by gathering His disciples and calling them to follow Him. In Jewish tradition, it was customary for rabbis to wait for their disciples to come to them. In fact, *Ben Sirach*, a Jewish Wisdom book, counseled a young man to take a rabbi to himself and "let your feet wear out his doorstep."[2] But Jesus didn't wait for His disciples to come to Him. Rather, He went to them and called them to Himself.

Walking by the Sea of Galilee, Jesus saw some fishermen at work. Their names are rightly famous today: Simon ("Peter"), his brother Andrew, James, the son of Zebedee, and his brother, John. Jesus boldly summons them to follow Him with the words, "Come, follow me and I will make you fishers of men" (Mark 1:17). As Dietrich Bonhoeffer notes, "The response of the disciples is an act of obedience, not a confession of faith in Jesus."[3] The disciples take

Jesus literally. They abandon their fathers and mothers, their servants and their nets, and march after Him. Jesus is the object of their faith, and this is immediately made real by their obedience. They live out an embodied life of discipleship.

Jesus' call to His disciples was totally gracious. Unlike many of our modern church recruitment techniques, Jesus' followers were never required to fill out an employment application, see the personnel committee, or have a searching interview with the senior pastor. Nor were they trained in theology. In fact, we know nothing of their qualifications for leadership apart from their willingness to follow Jesus.

Jesus reveals His desire to reach the masses by the disciples that He selects. He gathers them from the common people who were disdained by the religious elite. After all, who better to evangelize Galilee than working-class Galileans? They were the perfect contact point for Jesus' indigenous ministry—they had the ability to get His message to their relatives, friends, neighbors and business associates. But the disciples' destiny with Jesus lies far beyond their small world. Although they were ignorant of it at the time, the nations would one day stand before them.

What Jesus offers these men is Himself: "Follow me!" There is no greater privilege or passion than to be with Him.

LIVING OUT THE CALL

As Jesus gathers His core team, He becomes their pattern for life. He duplicates His ministry through them. He will make them more than they are. In the Jewish context, the rabbis not only taught the Torah (the Law), but they were also the "living" Torah. They wanted their disciples to learn by listening, watching and imitating their lives.

Rabbi Akiba, one of the great first-century rabbis, once told his disciples that he followed his rabbi, Joshua, into the toilet and "learned from him three good habits." Shocked, his disciple Ben Azzai asked, "How could you be so disrespectful of your teacher?" Akiba replied, "I considered everything part of the Torah [Law] and I needed to learn."[4] Indeed, Akiba's rabbi was a living Torah. To Akiba, even his rabbi's most private habits were a part of God's Law that were to be imitated.

Rich Nathan, pastor of the Columbus Vineyard in Ohio, pastors a church with about 8,000 in attendance on the weekends. He once told me that his congregation will do what they see the pastor doing. If the pastor leads people personally to Christ, so will his people. If the pastor publicly prays for the sick, so will his congregation. If the pastor goes to the poor, so will his people. I recently called Rich on his cell phone, and I was greeted by a lot of background noise. I asked, "Where are you, Rich?" He replied, "I'm under a bridge, praying for a homeless man." Here is a church invested in cross-cultural ministry that is reaching addicts, orphans, the unemployed, street-people, AIDS victims and the poor, and they are planting scores of churches. Why? Because they see it modeled in their pastor.

No wonder the Gospels are filled with what Jesus did as well as what He said. His disciples followed Him, went with Him, observed Him, and learned how to preach and minister from Him. They formed a community of brothers, and sisters (see Luke 8:1-3), gathered by Him to bring the Kingdom to the nations. As they submitted to the King, they submitted to His agenda. The Kingdom is at hand, within reach, and Jesus extended it through them, life by life, together. They joined Him in recruiting new disciples for the Kingdom who would become like them by hearing, seeing and doing what they do.

SHARING THE GOSPEL

The Kingdom, God's effective reign, moves out in time and space through Jesus. When Simon and Andrew followed Christ, God's reign moved into their lives. Together, they extended that reign further as more people entered the Kingdom through them. This is exactly the same for us. Jesus forms a new people for Himself, and we are called to join with Him in it. We enter the Kingdom now through the gate marked "Fishers of Men (and Women)."

Our task is to invest what God has done in our lives into the lives of others. Years ago, when I served as the pastor to college students at the Hollywood First Presbyterian Church, John Block, a sophomore from the University of Southern California, showed up. I couldn't miss him. He stood six feet, nine inches and played first-string center for the varsity basketball team. Since we were having our college retreat the next weekend, I invited John to come. He did, and we hung out together.

John shared that as a new Christian, he knew nothing about the faith. So I asked him if he would like to have one-on-one time with me when he returned to the campus. He hesitated for a moment and then replied, "Let's go for it." The next week, I went to his dorm, and we began to read Matthew's Gospel.

As we wrapped up our study that evening, I asked if we could pray out loud together. John had never done that before, but he was game. As I looked at him, I said, "Thanks, Lord, for bringing John and me together." I then announced that I had just prayed. What seemed spooky at first to him had been defused, and we prayed sentence prayers back and forth. We prayed for John's mom, his teammates and his roommate. Later, he walked me to my car. Before I jumped in, he said, "Don, I hope I can do this with someone else someday." Bingo! Right there I knew I had a winner.

He would reinvest my investment for the sake of the Kingdom.

What Jesus gave to me, I gave to John. Together, we brought young African-Americans from Harlem out to California to pursue their college education. At one point, we had Los Angeles's best after-season basketball with future NBA players in our church's cracker-box gym. We shared testimonies at halftime and took scores of young men on retreats.

John went on to play with the Los Angeles Lakers and other teams in the NBA for 10 years and then coached at several colleges. Each step of the way, he reinvested what the Lord had given him into the lives of others. After John retired from pro-basketball, he built a sports camp to reach kids with the gospel. The camp is now a multimillion dollar facility operated by Young Life. Today, John heads up a Christian gym in the heart of the inner city in San Diego and is deeply involved in mission work in Benin, Africa.

Likewise, we can make an investment in those around us. Moms and dads, invest what God has given you into the lives of your children. Francis MacNutt, a former Roman Catholic priest and a leader in the charismatic renewal movement, often asked people if they could remember as children their parents praying hands-on for their healing. Perhaps 5 percent of the women and about 0 percent of the men ever answered in the affirmative. Share the gospel with your children. Read the Bible with them. Pray with them. Let your children become involved with you in Kingdom ministry.

Teachers, invest in your students. Students, invest in your class-mates. Businessmen and businesswomen, invest in your employees or fellow workers. Ask God to show you who to spend one-on-one time with. Build friendships. Make the commitment. Read the Bible together and start praying with your family and friends. Jump over your fears and launch out. As mentioned before, John Wimber spoke of commitment as time, money and energy. Give all of this away for the Kingdom. Let Jesus get your focus off yourself and onto others for their sakes, His sake and, truly, your sake as well.

Of course, as we follow Jesus, we may wonder where He is going. What does it mean to be called to Kingdom ministry? What does it mean for the Kingdom to be within reach?

CHAPTER 7

RELEASE TO THE CAPTIVES

According to current church-growth principles, if Jesus were to plant a church today, He would begin by canvassing the neighborhood to find those interested in hearing Him preach. He would send out a mailing announcing His new church. He would identify the felt needs of people and plan to meet them. He would instruct His disciples how to be "seeker friendly," or how to identify emotional and relational needs that He could address. All of these are helpful ideas on how to start a new church. Yet Jesus began His ministry by casting out demons. Francis MacNutt has said that if you want to start a worldwide ministry, just heal a few people.

As we have seen, Jesus is the anointed Davidic Warrior-King. Jesus battled Satan in the wilderness and gathered His first followers to launch His movement. His name tells us a major part of His story: "Jesus" means "Joshua," or "Deliverer." Just as Joshua led Israel into the Promised Land to cleanse it of pagan idols, Jesus entered the Promised Land to cleanse it of unclean spirits—demons that sought to afflict, possess and destroy God's good creation. In the Exodus, Joshua extended God's kingdom throughout the land. Jesus does the same.

Mark describes this campaign in his Gospel. At the start of Jesus' ministry, everything appeared to be safe and normal. Like a good rabbi, Jesus went into the synagogue in Capernaum on the Sabbath and began to teach (see Mark 1:21). Yet it soon became apparent that He was different from other rabbis. He addressed the crowd, unlike the teachers of the law. He spoke with direct, naked authority and didn't use footnotes (unlike most rabbis, who referred to other rabbis in a chain of tradition). His message certainly included the fact that the Kingdom was at hand or within reach.

But the point of Mark's story is that when Jesus arrived on the scene, all hell was unleashed. As Jesus taught, suddenly a demon (literally, "an unclean spirit") manifested itself. Using a man's voice, it addressed Jesus, saying, "What do you want with us, Jesus of Nazareth? Have you come to destroy us? I know who you are—the Holy One of God" (Mark 1:24). Jesus responded decisively. He commanded the demon, "Be quiet" (literally "be muzzled," as if He were restraining a mad dog) and then expelled it by saying, "Come out of him!" As a result, the evil spirit shook the man violently and came out of him with a shriek (see Mark 1:26).

This amazed the crowd. Church was never like this! Demons were subject to Jesus. The kingdom of God was in their midst and the enemy's agents were now on the run. As a result, the news about Jesus traveled like wildfire, spreading "quickly over the whole region of Galilee" (Mark 1:28). The Kingdom moved out from Jesus and His core followers to this demonized man and to others coming to faith in the synagogue.

So what are we to make of this?

THE WORLDVIEW CRISIS

For us, this type of encounter provokes a worldview crisis. Demons don't fit our modern (or even post-modern) perception of reality. Today, many scholars try to explain away the fact that people in the biblical accounts were demon possessed by labeling them as personality disorders. The idea is that because of the unscientific worldview in ancient time, what was really a psychotic disorder was seen as a demon possession. Jesus, accommodating Himself to this primitive way of thinking, simply brought those suffering from this psychosis to their senses.

But was this really the case? What if the New Testament worldview is right? What if Satan is a real spiritual enemy who oppresses us and seeks to possess us? What if Paul was dead-on when he wrote, "Put on the full armor of God so that you can take your stand against the devil's schemes . . . For our struggle is not against flesh and blood, but against the rulers, against the authorities, against the powers of this dark world and against the spiritual forces of evil in the heavenly realms" (Eph. 6:11-12)? What if Luther was more perceptive than the modern mind when he wrote, "And tho' this world with devils filled, Doth threaten to undo us, We will not fear for God has willed, His truth to triumph through us"?[1]

Most evangelicals agree that Satan and demons are real, but they usually consign their influence to the first century. They reason that because Jesus defeated the devil, people today have nothing more to do with demons. This explanation seems to work until we hear missionaries and church leaders report on encounters with demons in Africa, Asia and South America. The evidence streams into our major seminaries from credible witnesses that demons are still active in our world today. Then we learn of the whole underbelly of Western culture with its surviving pagan cults, satanic churches, witchcraft, astrology, mediums, ghosts, séances, and a host of other dark practices, including animal and child sacrifice.

Is all of this primitive illusion? Or is this evidence of dark powers invading our lives and, at times, even our sanity? In fact, Satan and demons are real. To enter the kingdom of God is to be delivered from the kingdom of the evil one. But God's kingdom is both in the "now" and "yet to come." We are not made perfect at the point of our conversion—we still bear the effects of our own sin and the enemy's inroads made against us personally and generationally. While we are delivered from Satan's domain, we may still be subject to his infestation or oppression (which usually must be dealt with specifically).

The New Testament simply calls this "demonization." Demonic contact points may include participation in cults, childhood abuse, addiction or a family history of witchcraft or other occult practices. Paul warns that even unresolved anger may give Satan entry: "'In your anger do not sin': Do not let the sun go down while you are still angry, and do not give the devil a foothold" (Eph. 4:26-27). Demons connect with us when we give them the moral or legal right to be there. We keep them there by hiding behind our denial and shame.

Throughout most of Church history—and among most Christ-ians in the world today (apart from our semi-secularized Western churches)—Satan was perceived as being real, and Christians were perceived as being in a real spiritual battle. Ramsay MacMillen, Professor of Classics at Yale University, in his work *Christianizing the Roman Empire, AD 100-400*, stated that the Church converted Rome basically by casting out demons.[2] In missiological terms, these were power encounters—a contest between Jesus and the gods, goddesses (masking demons) and the lesser spirits of the Roman Empire. When no pagan priest or medium could deliver people, the oppressed came to the Church, were set free, and converted to the highest power, Jesus. So over the gate into the Kingdom stands this banner: "Welcome to the War."

CASTING OUT DEMONS

What can we gather from the account in Mark 1:21 of Jesus freeing the demon-possessed man in the synagogue? We learn that apart from having a spiritual, dark enemy, there are also demons with real personalities in the world today. Demons come to challenge spiritual authority. They often manifest in the powerful presence of Jesus and His followers (and the power of the Spirit), and they may especially manifest in a synagogue or church service where people are worshiping the living God.

In the presence of Jesus (and His followers), the demons realized that their doom had come, so they used the vocal cords of those they infested to speak out against Christ: "Have you come to destroy us?" (Mark 1:24). Demons had a supernatural knowledge of Jesus: "I know who you are—the Holy One of God!" (v. 24). However, they were forced to yield to Jesus' authority. Jesus didn't debate them, for He knew that there was no reason to argue with them or believe anything that they said. He simply silenced them with the words "Be quiet [muzzled]" (v. 25) and then drove them out with the sheer authority of His word: "Come out of him!" (v. 25). When the demons departed, they left the man with physical convulsions and noise: "The evil spirit shook the man violently and came out of him with a shriek" (v. 26).

As Jesus' disciples watched this event occur, they had no worldview (or "paradigm") shift. Everyone in Galilee at that time believed in demons and regularly saw them at work. However, the disciples realized that what they now had was the One who had the authority and power to deal with the demons. The disciples soon were on a steep learning curve as Jesus began to show them how to set people free. Later, Jesus would send them out to do the same: "He appointed twelve—designating them apostles—that they might be with him and that he might send them out to preach and to have authority to drive out demons" (Mark 3:14-15).

The practice of casting out demons in the name and authority of Jesus continued on into the Early Church. In Acts 16:18, Luke describes a situation in which Paul delivered a slave girl in Philippi: "Finally Paul became so troubled that he turned around and said to the spirit [of divination], 'In the name of Jesus Christ I command you to come out of her!' At that moment the spirit left her." The second-century Church father Irenaeus noted that casting out demons was also a prevalent practice at that time:

> Wherefore, also, those who are in truth, His [Jesus'] disci-
> ples, receiving grace from him, do in his name perform [mir-
> acles], so as to promote the welfare of other men, according
> to the gift that each one has received from him. For some do
> certainly and truly drive out devils, so that those who have
> thus been cleansed from evil spirits frequently both believe
> [in Christ], and join themselves to the church.[3]

Lance Pittluck, pastor of the Anaheim Vineyard Church, once observed that seeing demons leave a person is a life-changing experience. It was for me as well. Up until the mid-1980s, I had only a formal belief in the devil. After all, I was an evangelical. Then I received a call from a musician friend, who I will call Johnny. Johnny became a Christian in high school and was filled with the Holy Spirit. Although he had been addicted to drugs since early adolescence, he stopped using them for a year after his conversion, and then relapsed. Now in his mid-20s, he was dying of cocaine addiction.

When I met up with Johnny, he was skin and bones, unable to hold a job, and using every night. He would go up on cocaine and come down on Jack Daniels. We saw each other daily and prayed a lot, and I informally became his sponsor. But nothing worked. He was still in the uncontrolled force of his addiction. I knew that he would probably die soon. In desperation, I called Joe Ozawa, a psychologist friend of mine in private practice in Los Angeles.

Joe graduated from Harvard and had received his Ph.D. from the University of Southern California. Because I respected him, I had to think twice when he asked me if I had ever prayed for Johnny for deliverance from demons. Frankly, it had never crossed my mind. I had no concept of this, but I was desperate. Joe said that he would be in San Diego (where I lived) later in the week, and told me to ask Johnny if he wanted us to pray for him. I hesitated, but then I thought, *What do I have to lose?* So I gingerly raised the subject to Johnny the next time we met together. To my surprise, Johnny said that he saw a host of demons leaving his body in a dream two weeks ago. This was God's setup. Johnny was ready for us to help him.

Joe, Johnny and I met the next Thursday night in the offices of the Presbyterian Church, where I pastored. We prayed for several hours. Johnny knew the names or types of the demons that needed to go. We bound all other spirits, welcomed the Holy Spirit, and then covered the room with the blood of Jesus through prayer. We started with the weakest spirits, cutting off their communication with each other, and then worked our way to the strongest. As the demons left, some slipped out quietly, but others went out noisily. Some challenged us or threatened us.

At the end of the evening, we were exhausted but at peace. The next morning I called Johnny, as was my custom, to see how he was doing. He said, "Don, for the first time in years, I have no desire to do cocaine." He was free! Many battles and much healing lay ahead for him, but he later graduated from college and became a drug counselor in a private practice.

Since that night, I have seen many demons go. Francis MacNutt estimates that about 30 percent of all people in the pews need some kind of deliverance.[4] But where can they get it? The answer is simple: from Jesus and His disciples.

PREPARE FOR BATTLE

In the first five chapters of Mark's Gospel, there are 22 references to Satan or demons. Jesus says that He had come to bind the strong man (Satan) and plunder his house (see Mark 3:27). In Luke 11:20, Jesus says, "But if I drive out demons by the finger of God, then the kingdom of God has come to you." In Acts, Peter tells a Roman officer how "God anointed Jesus of Nazareth with the Holy Spirit and power, and how he went around doing good and healing all who were under the power of the devil, because God was with him" (10:38). In Romans, Paul says, "The God of peace will soon crush Satan under your feet" (16:20). John says, "The reason the Son of God appeared was to destroy the devil's work" (1 John 3:8). This is the Kingdom come.

Being practical, we need to know that in Jesus' name we have authority over all unclean spirits. While we are not to go looking for them, we need to be ready for battle. How do we prepare? Consider the following:

- **Arm for Battle.** Paul tells us to put on the whole armor of God: the helmet of salvation, the breastplate of righteousness, the girdle of truth, the shoes of the gospel of peace, the sword of the Spirit and the shield of faith (see Eph. 6:10-17). Simply put, we need to cover ourselves with the gospel.

- **Know the Word of God.** Jesus defeated the devil with Scripture, and so must we. We need to learn key verses about our authority in Christ and His conquest of the enemy.

· **Be Wise About Your Vulnerability to Spiritual Attack.**
Take a moral inventory. Confess all known sins and keep your
confession current (see 1 John 1:9).

· **Build Accountable Relationships.** Build relationships with
a small circle of intimate friends who know your dark side
and your struggles. Ask these friends to pray actively for you
and your healing, and have them exhort and challenge you.

· **Renounce All Idols.** Renounce all participation in the occult
or cults. Renounce all addictions. Ask God to heal your past
pain and fill the hole in your soul with His Spirit.

· **Forgive All.** Forgive all those who have hurt you, gossiped
about you and sinned against you. Receive forgiveness for
your anger and resentment toward them and toward yourself.

· **Pray for Protection Against the Enemy.** Ask intercessors to
pray for you (see Eph. 6:18-20).

· **Pray for Discernment of Spirits.** Pray that the Holy Spirit
will give you prophetic insight into the spiritual realm and
for the names of specific demons that need to leave (see
1 Cor. 12:10).

· **Bind Evil Spirits.** Learn how to bind evil spirits in Jesus'
name through prayer and send them to Jesus to be dealt with
by Him.

· **Submit to Spiritual Authority.** Minister deliverance in a
team.

- **Clean Up.** Clean up your heart, your house and yourself after encounters with the enemy. Learn cleansing prayers, and pray them!

- **Seek Help.** Acquire good resources on this difficult ministry.

Remember, we need to stay committed to community. In Ephesians 6, Paul called the whole Church (not just individuals) to arms, described his needs, and then asked for corporate prayer. We must stand in this battle together. An isolated Christian is a defeated Christian. As they say in Alcoholics Anonymous, "When you isolate, you're sick."

Let me offer a final word of caution: Before we deal directly with issues of deliverance, we need to learn the symptoms of affliction and ask for the Holy Spirit's discernment. A Baptist pastor once called me about one of my former students, who had become wracked with anxiety, phobic and immobilized. He had decided that the student needed deliverance and asked if I would pray for him. Of course, I agreed.

So the pastor brought the student in to see me. We talked a bit about his symptoms and the onset of his anxiety (I was praying for discernment). After some time, I became convinced that there were no demons present. So I had the student make an appointment with a psychiatrist and get on appropriate medication. All of his symptoms left in a brief period of time, and he was able to go back to work. Medication was his miracle. Remember, God is both Creator and Redeemer. As Creator, He gives us doctors and medicine. As Redeemer, He gives us the gospel and the authority of Jesus through the power and gifts of the Spirit. They do not contradict but complement each other.

Jesus calls us into Kingdom ministry to set the captives free. The Gospel of Mark tells us that after Jesus taught the disciples how to cast out demons in His name, "He sent them out two by two and gave them authority over evil spirits" (Mark 6:7). The result? "They went out and preached that people should repent. They drove out many demons and anointed many sick people with oil and healed them" (Mark 6:12-13).

This was no isolated event. This was their entrance into Kingdom ministry. We must expect no less!

CHAPTER 8

HEALING THE SICK

Jesus came not only to drive out demons but also to heal the sick. His Kingdom ministry restores this fallen creation. Disease is under challenge by Him.

After delivering the man in the synagogue from an unclean spirit, and with His disciples tagging along (probably thunderstruck by now), Jesus then went to Simon (Peter) and Andrew's house for supper. Peter's mother-in-law was in bed with a fever. Jesus approached her, took her hand and helped her up. Mark reports, "The fever left her and she began to wait upon them" (1:31).

Notice here that Jesus *took her hand*. Healing by touch was common to Jesus. Here is Luke's summary: "He [Jesus] went down . . . and stood on a level place. A large crowd of his disciples was there and a great number of people . . . who had come to hear him and to be healed of their diseases. Those troubled by evil spirits were cured, and the people all tried to touch him, because power was coming from him and healing them all" (6:17-19).

Again, when a woman with an issue of blood touched Jesus in a crowd, He stopped and asked, "Who touched me?" Bemused, His disciples pointed to the crowd all around Him, but Jesus replied, "Someone touched me; I know that power has gone out from me"

(Luke 8:46) Clearly, as Jesus was filled with the Spirit, His touch transmitted His power and people were healed. Later, when Peter healed a crippled man at the Jerusalem Temple gate called "Beautiful," he commanded, "In the name of Jesus Christ of Nazareth, walk." Then Peter, taking the man by the right hand, "helped him up, and instantly the man's feet and ankles became strong. He jumped to his feet and began to walk. Then he went with them into the temple courts, walking and jumping, and praising God" (Acts 3:7-8).

THE TOUCH OF THE HOLY SPIRIT

John Wimber, leader of the Vineyard Movement for many years, heard the Lord tell him early on that he was to teach his church how to heal the sick. He did this for several months with no results. After training his members to pray, they not only didn't see any healings, but they also caught many of the diseases themselves. John was deeply discouraged, but he still felt that God had told him to do this.

One early Monday morning, a friend whose wife had the flu called John and asked him to come over for what John believed to be a pastoral call. On John's arrival, however, the friend asked him to pray for his wife's healing. As John tells it, he went into her bedroom and she looked terrible—she was flushed with fever. With about zero faith, he went to her bed, held her hand and prayed a perfunctory healing prayer. He started to explain to her that God doesn't heal everybody when, suddenly, she was out of her bed like a shot.

Everything changed. She was a new person. She put on her bathrobe, combed her hair and made John a cup of coffee. Later, he walked to his car elated, saying, "I got one, Lord, I got one!" This was the beginning of John Wimber's international healing ministry.[1]

I had a similar experience at the Toronto Airport Church in Canada. I was there for a series of meetings, and while exiting the building late at night, tired from praying for scores of people, a woman caught me. She took me over to her friend who was stretched out on several folding chairs, looking sick as a dog. She had the flu and asked that I pray for her healing. I did so, mostly out of obedience. I took her hand, asked Jesus to heal her, and then left.

The next day, a radiant woman stopped me and asked if I remembered praying for her the previous night. I searched my memory. She announced that she was the woman with the flu. She had been totally healed! Her face and bearing had changed so dramatically that I could hardly recognize her, but she was the woman. Like Peter's mother-in-law, Jesus had healed her through a short prayer and the touch of the Holy Spirit through me.

PRAYING FOR HEALING

In Mark 1:40-45, Jesus encountered a leper who said to Him, "If you are willing, you can make me clean" (v. 40). Would Jesus heal him? "Filled with compassion, Jesus reached out his hand and touched the man. 'I am willing,' he said. 'Be clean!' Immediately the leprosy left him and he was cured" (vv. 41-42).

Notice that Jesus' touch was joined by a prayer of command. Jesus often spoke to disease in the same way He spoke to demons, and people were healed. His Spirit can give us the same authority and grace. We are not to follow a formula, but to listen for His leading. We can learn to pray for the sick and participate in Jesus' Kingdom ministry, restoring His rule over sickness and disease.

John Wimber developed a fivefold healing model that is simple and effective when empowered by the Holy Spirit. First, an interview is conducted with the sick person in which he or she is asked for some preliminary background and what needs to be healed. This is not meant to be a counseling session—the person simply identifies his or her issue for prayer.

Second, those who are praying for the individual ask Jesus how they are to pray and then wait for Him to answer. He may give them an impression, a picture, a word or some other direction that may take them deeper than the initial request. If they do not receive anything from God as they pray and listen, they then base their prayer on the person's request and move to intercession or even a prayer of command, speaking directly to the illness or disease.

Third, those who are praying for healing invite the Holy Spirit to come, and then they watch with their eyes open for evidence of His presence. They may actually see signs of what God is doing (physical clues such as a sheen on the person's face, muscles relaxing, eyelids fluttering, body moving, gentle falling backward). With the person's approval, they may also lay hands on him or her appropriately, believing that the Spirit's power is often transmitted through touch.

Fourth, after praying for a bit, the person is asked if he or she feels anything: "Is the pain any better?" "Are you getting symptom relief?" "Are you aware of the Holy Spirit touching you?" If there is improvement, they continue to pray, but if there is no change, they also continue to pray (often, when people pray a second or third time, things begin to happen). If the person is healed, those who are doing the praying can stop.

Fifth, the people who have prayed for the individual have a brief conversation, answering questions such as "Where do you go from here?" They may recommend continuing prayer for difficult illnesses, such as cancer or heart disease or rheumatoid arthritis. They may recommend that the person join a small group or return again for prayer the following week, or they may even feel led to have more personal involvement with the person.[2]

Praying for healing is always a faith-adventure. It requires listening, patience and sensitivity to the Spirit. We should always remember when we are praying for someone that *we* can't heal anyone. Only Jesus heals. This is His work, not ours. We are simply an instrument of His kingdom at the point of prayer.

SIGN OF THE KINGDOM

As Francis MacNutt states, most healing today is typically "more or less."[3] It is not simply all or nothing—out of the wheelchair and down the aisle. So it is important for us to keep on praying as long as we see some improvement or results. In large healing services, Francis says that about 5 percent of people receive a miraculous healing, while in smaller settings, 60 to 70 percent find their condition improved as people continue to pray for them.

Remember, we live between the present and future coming of the Kingdom. Not everyone we pray for will be healed, but some will because of the power of the Spirit, our obedience, their faith and the sovereign grace of God. However, most people, if we keep on praying for them, will get better. This keeps us going and growing in this aspect of Kingdom ministry.

Jesus the King is on the move. His rule and reign are overcoming the effects of Satan and sin in our broken world. As it was then, so it is today. To stay in the healing ministry for a lifetime, we must resolve to live in tension. Not everyone we pray for will be healed, just as not everyone we witness to will be converted. We minister, as we have seen, in the present breakthroughs of the kingdom of God on this earth. A perfectionist theology (one that believes everyone we pray for will be healed) will ultimately drive us out of business. A cessationist theology (one that believes all healing ended in the first century) will keep us from ever going into business. But if we continue to pray with Jesus' compassion and the Spirit's anointing, we will stay in business.

Again, faith—and, sometimes, desperation—will release God's power. Every healing (physical, emotional and spiritual) is a sign of the Kingdom. God is restoring His fallen creation in body, soul and spirit. We enter the Kingdom through the gate marked "Heal the Sick." Come on in!

CHAPTER 9

THE SECRET OF KINGDOM MINISTRY

Archibald Hart, Professor of Psychology at Fuller Theological Seminary, speaking to a group of pastors, once said that we exhaust ourselves on Sunday and then crash on Monday. We think, *I am so depressed; the devil is really after me. He is attacking me because I really went for it yesterday.* Dr. Hart responds, "We aren't being attacked. We are just coming off our addiction to our own adrenalin." Whether this is fully the case (Satan will exploit our weaknesses), Dr. Hart has a point. We all get depleted and need to be recharged.

So how do we find the strength to persevere in ministry? Again, Jesus is our King and also our model. In Mark 1:35, after a long day (and night) of ministry, Jesus was out early: "Very early in the morning, while it was still dark, Jesus got up, left the house and went off to a solitary place, where he prayed." If Jesus is our model, then we need to follow Him to a solitary place and have Him teach us to pray.

A deep secret of Jesus' Kingdom ministry was His relationship with the Father. When Jesus came into the world, their unbroken intimacy was now revealed in His incarnate life. Not only was Jesus continually dependent upon the Father, but He also enjoyed profound communion with Him. While they were in constant inter-action, Jesus needed to withdraw and pray. We need to do this, too. Here are some simple points for us as Christ followers.

First, Jesus started His day with the Father. This was His first pri-ority. Psychologists observe that the way we start our day will deter-mine how we get through it. If we wake up with criticism and com-plaint, this will last throughout the day. If we wake up with love and affection, this too will last throughout the day. The "opening bell" radically changes how we will feel and function. So Jesus began His day with the Father.

Although we know actually very little about Jesus' prayer life, we do know that it was intimate, dynamic and full of glory. Remember, Jesus sought the Father, who said (and says), "This is my Son, whom I love; with him I am well pleased" (Matt. 3:17). At the start of your day, through Jesus hear the Father speak these words to you as His son or daughter.

Second, Jesus often went away to be alone with the Father. In my own situation, I have found that I need to be alone for heartfelt, self-disclosing prayer to happen. When I am alone, I can pray out loud without worrying that I am being overheard. Spoken prayer keeps my mind from wandering and keeps me focused. It also allows me to ver-balize my emotions and get them out freely before the Lord. I can assume physical postures that express my heart. I can sing or make up songs to the Lord, free from the judgments or approval of others.

No wonder Jesus says, "And when you pray, do not be like the hypocrites, for they love . . . to be seen by men [and women]. I tell you the truth, they have received their reward in full [namely, the applause of the crowd or the congregation—that's it!]. But when you pray, go into your room, close the door and pray to your Father, who is unseen. Then your Father, who sees what is done in secret, will reward you" (Matt. 6:5-6). As it is with Jesus, so it is with us.

Third, Jesus finds a special place to pray, a solitary place. In the same way, to build our relationship with the Lord, we need to find a solitary place to seek Him. We need quiet places—if possible, out of doors. Nature will enhance our desire to pray. One of my favorite things to do is to walk on the beach in the early morning, let the tide lap at my feet, hear the seagulls squawk, feel the wind on my face, and look to the horizon with a new sense of the beauty and majesty of God.

KINGDOM PRAYING

Although, as we have said, we don't know much about how Jesus prayed to the Father (John 17 is the great exception), we do know how He wants us to pray. He gives us the model in the so-called Lord's Prayer, or the "Our Father" prayer. Sadly, this teaching has been so largely dumbed down by the Church that it has lost its sense of the Kingdom.

When Jesus' disciples came to Him to ask for their special prayer, He responded by teaching them to pray the Kingdom. This was not meant to be a rote formula, sanitized in redundant Church liturgy, but a model for our own praying. It puts the power of intercession into our Kingdom ministry. Let's briefly consider its movement.

Our Father in Heaven

First, the address: "Our Father in heaven" (Matt. 6:9). Jesus shows us that the sovereign King, radiant in holiness, magnificent in majesty and full of grace, is also our loving Father. He is our *Abba*, which in Jesus' spoken tongue, Aramaic, means "Daddy"; or, as *The Living Bible* renders it, "Father, dear Father" (see Rom. 8:15). Jesus comes to make the Father known to us and to draw us into their eternal exclusive love relationship. Because of Him (and in Him), we start our prayer with, "Our Father."

But this Father is also in heaven. We are not to confuse our earthly fathers with our heavenly Father. As the great King, He is above us in eternal glory. As our Father, He is with us in His Son. To use theological language, He is both transcendent and imminent. Moreover, He is in us by His Spirit. We are in awe of Him and in love with Him. Jesus alone teaches us to address the living God as Father. With this, He draws us into the very life of the Trinity itself.

Hallowed Be Your Name

After identifying the God to whom we pray and acknowledging that we are in the presence of our King and Father who is ready to hear and act on our behalf, we begin our petitions. With the first petition, "Hallowed be your name" (Matt. 6:9), we simply ask for God's name to be set apart, protected from profanity, honored, exalted and kept sacred. In this passage in Matthew, Jesus shows us that when we start petitioning our heavenly Father (who is the great King), our primary concern should be with Him, not ourselves. Jesus writes His burning passion for God's name on our hearts. It is to be kept unique and totally different from all other names.

Unfortunately, our ears are often filled with lesser names: Prince William, Martha Stewart, Donald Trump, Paris Hilton, Tony Blair, George Bush, Bill Gates, Tom Cruise, Brittany Spears, Paul McCartney, Hillary Rodham Clinton, to name just a few. We know the names of tyrants, pop stars, political leaders, business moguls, technocrats, media personalities and the Royals. These names overshadow the one name worthy of our worship, our devotion and our fame—the very name of God Himself.

So we ask God to do what no human can do: make His own name holy, hallowed, separated and sanctified. As we pray this, we are in the will of God. This prayer will be answered. One day, every knee will bow and every tongue will confess that "Jesus is Lord, to the glory of God the Father" (Phil. 2:11). In this age, God suffers heresy, profanity and unbelief, but He will glorify Himself alone in the coming Day of Justice.

But we are not only praying into the future—the "not yet" when God will vindicate Himself—but we are also praying into the now, the "already." We are asking God to honor His name and make it great in our time and space through the advancement of His kingdom. As I write this, there is good news: The knowledge of God and the gospel of His Son are burning across our planet. Today, there are at least 80 million Christians in China, most of them in the underground churches.[1] Let us pray, then, for God to vindicate His name through His Son. Let us pray for the name of Jesus to be lifted up in our age, our culture, our media and our public discourse, and pray that this will happen in every culture, every tongue, tribe and nation around the world. "Hallowed be Your name."

Your Kingdom Come

Next, we pray for the Kingdom to come. In the Lord's Prayer, Jesus identified the Kingdom as the will of God. The lines "Your kingdom come/Your will be done" (Matt. 6:10) parallel and complement each other. As we have seen, Satan revolted against the will of God, corrupted our race, and corrupted the earth. God intervened, calling Israel and sending His Son to restore His Kingdom reign, His will, on this planet.

Furthermore, Jesus shows us that the will of God is presently done "in heaven," that whole other dimension of reality where God is enthroned before a sea of angels, adored and honored in unceasing worship. There His sovereignty is unchallenged: sin, sorrow and darkness are unknown and perfect power is joined with perfect love and perfect justice. So we ask for heaven to invade Earth. We ask for the eternal Kingdom of righteousness, mercy and glory to come to us in the here and now. "As in heaven, so on earth."

This petition acknowledges that God is King; His heavenly kingdom fully manifests His will. But it also implies that His kingdom has not yet been fully established on Earth. So we pray for God's intervention. Out of His amazing love, He invites us to participate in His work. Again, we are asking God to do His own heart's desire. Jesus is teaching us to pray for exactly the message and mission He brought. So we join our prayers with His as we cry out for His kingdom to come in the here and now.

In the larger biblical context, as we pray for the Kingdom, we pray for the coming of the Spirit, the overthrow of Satan's counterfeit kingdom, the poor to be evangelized, the outsiders to become insiders, the demonized to be set free, the sick to be healed, and for God's justice to rule and overrule all the structures and powers of evil.

Be warned: As we pray this prayer in its Kingdom context, God will answer and draft us into His Kingdom mission. Our lives will never be the same. As Jesus promises, we will have tribulation in this world (see John 16:33). The armies of hell will launch their strikes against us. But the armies of heaven are with us, and even if we are chosen to walk through martyrdom, we will prevail. "Blessed are the dead who die in the Lord from now on. 'Yes,' says the Spirit, 'they will rest from their labor, for their deeds will follow them'" (Rev. 14:13).

Give Us Tomorrow's Bread Today
Fourth, we pray, "Give us tomorrow's bread today." I know that this translation will surprise you, but it is accurate. Traditionally, we are taught that we are to pray for our "daily bread"—a phrasing that has probably done the most to sanitize this prayer. But we are not simply asking for God to meet our daily needs—Jesus is teaching us to pray for "tomorrow's bread." What does this refer to? It is the

Messianic Bread. This is the fulfillment of the manna, or bread, that God provided for the Israelites in their Exodus journey through the wilderness. Part of Israel's hope for the future was that in the final Exodus—the wrap-up—God would send bread again from heaven. In John's Gospel, Jesus identifies Himself as the "Bread of Life" (John 6:35). He has come down from heaven to give life to the world. He says to the Jews that their fathers ate manna in the wilderness and died, but if they eat of Him, they will live forever.

So when we pray, "Give us tomorrow's [the Kingdom's] Bread," we pray "Send the Messiah" or "Send the heavenly Bread." In a Kingdom context, this makes perfect sense. We ask God to send His Messiah now, "today." As we ask for this, Jesus is our answer. But He is not only the one who has come; He is also the one who is coming again. So we continue to pray this prayer down through the ages, knowing that it has already partially been fulfilled: Jesus has come (past); through His Spirit He is with us now (present); and one day, He will come in glory (future). Then this petition will be fully answered.

Forgive Us Our Sins

Fifth, we pray, "Forgive us our sins [debts, trespasses] as we forgive those who have sinned against us" (Matt. 6:12). Forgiveness, like the Kingdom come and the Messianic Bread today, is God's promise to us when He comes in glory and wraps up all things. When the Kingdom comes, mercy will triumph over justice. When the Kingdom comes, all things will be reconciled to the holy God. Forgiveness is a central fact of our salvation.

We know from the gospel that forgiveness is all God's work. It is free, unmerited, unconditional and totally gracious. But this petition creates a problem. It is qualified. We are to pray that God will forgive us our sins, just as we forgive the sins of others. So, if we forgive others a little, will God also forgive us a little? Do we control

His mercy? Is His mercy dependent on what we do, how gracious we are, or how forgiving we become? Hardly.

True, Jesus does say that as we forgive so will we be forgiven, which raises the question, How much do we want God to forgive us? If we respond, "Fully, completely," then we must forgive in the same way. The true Christian has no alternative. When we come to the Cross, we don't receive what we deserve. We deserve punishment, yet we receive pardon. Because this has happened to us, it must happen through us to others. As John Arnott once said as he led new Christians in prayer, "We receive the gift that we do not deserve, and we give the gift that others do not deserve." It is simple: The forgiven forgive freely and fully.

To illustrate this fact, Jesus told a story about a manager who owed his master a huge sum of money (see Matt. 18:21-35). Because the manager was unable to pay, his master had mercy on him and forgave the whole debt. But the manager then turned right around and forced a servant who owed him a few pennies to pay up. The servant was unable to pay, but rather than forgive this paltry sum, the manager threw the servant and his family into debtor's prison. When the manager's master heard of this, he reversed his decision and threw the manager himself into prison. Why? Because though he had been forgiven much, he refused to forgive little. From this story, we learn that we are to forgive as God forgives: fully, from our hearts.

In the Kingdom, forgiveness always triumphs. The cross wins. We are fully reconciled to God and to each other. Forgiveness then heals our hearts, restores our relationships, lifts away our guilt, blocks Satan's designs to hold us in bondage (the prison of our own unforgiveness) and sets us free from crippling psychosomatic illnesses (such as migraine headaches, arthritis, insomnia and a weakened immune system that can trigger cancer and other life-threatening diseases).

Lead Us Not into Temptation

Sixth, we pray that God will "lead us not into temptation, but deliver us from the evil one [Satan]" (Matt. 6:13). Of course, we know that God does not tempt us—this is the work of our own lusts and the enemy (see Jas. 1:13; 1 Thess. 3:5). So what can this petition mean?

The temptation that Jesus refers to here is the final birth pangs—the final holocaust, the final hour of trial—before the Kingdom fully comes with His glorious return. The parallel petition makes this clear: "But deliver us from the evil *one* [not "evil," as in an abstraction]" (Matt. 6:13). In the final hours of our history, Satan will rage against planet Earth. He will seek to destroy God's people and God's Church. He will fill graves with our corpses and rivers with our blood. Like a hooked game fish, his final lunge will be his hardest before he is gaffed and pulled into the boat.

So we pray for protection: "Lead us not into the final hour of testing/Deliver us from Satan." In the book of Revelation, Jesus promised the church in Philadelphia, "Since you have kept my command to endure patiently, I will also keep you from the hour of trial that is going to come upon the whole world to test those who live on the earth" (Rev. 3:10). This is the promise that we also ask to be fulfilled for us. But this petition is not simply for the future—it's also for today. Because God's kingdom is within reach, we are in the battle now, up to our ears. We need to pray constantly for deliverance from the enemy. Jesus Himself intercedes for us: "My prayer is not that you take them out of the world but that you protect them from the evil one" (John 17:15).

For Yours Is the Kingdom, the Power, and the Glory

Matthew's Gospel adds a final ascription to the Lord's Prayer: "For yours is the kingdom, the power, and the glory forever. Amen." While this is not in the earliest Greek manuscripts, it is certainly a fitting conclusion for Kingdom praying.

As Jesus' followers, He gives us the structure and outline for our prayers. We are to address the living God as our loving Father in heaven. We are to ask Him to vindicate His name, bring His kingdom from heaven to Earth both in the future and in the present, feed us with the Messianic Bread (Jesus), forgive us fully as we forgive fully, protect us in the final battle (and all the attacks that lead up to it), and deliver us from the devil.

Build your own prayers on these themes. Meditate on them and let the Holy Spirit pray them through you. Expect God to answer these prayers in your life of discipleship. Record the answers as they come. Remember them and be grateful.

A LIFE OF PRAYER

Years ago, I inherited the college ministry of Hollywood First Presbyterian Church, founded by Henrietta Mears, one of the most significant Christian leaders of the twentieth century. When she came to Hollywood, she expanded the Sunday School program at the church from 600 to 6,000 in a few short years. She was the inspiration behind Bill and Vonette Bright's founding of Campus Crusade for Christ. She started Forest Home, one of the largest Christian conference centers in the nation. She revolutionized Sunday School curriculum with Gospel Light Press.

Miss Mears personally led countless students to Christ in her living room near the UCLA campus. More than 400 young men from her college class went into the Presbyterian ministry along with countless other students who went into ministry in other denominations and mission enterprises. What was her secret? Prayer undergirded by boundless faith. I recall one of her spiritual sons, Louis Evans, Jr., the founding pastor of the Bel Air Presbyterian Church, saying that when Miss Mears prayed, she reached up and shook the throne of heaven.

I learned that secret the first Sunday I taught her college class. After I concluded the lesson, an elderly woman came to me and said, "I am Mother Atwater. When Miss Mears came to Hollywood 30 years ago, I told her that if she would teach students, I would sit in the back and pray. I have done this every Sunday. Now that you are here, I will sit in the back and pray for you." I teared up and realized that I was now ready to be catapulted on the same secret that carried her over the years. Remember, we enter the Kingdom through the gate marked "Pray, Always Pray."

CHAPTER 10

EXTENDING THE KINGDOM

For most of us, the Christian life becomes settled, predictable and routine. We go to church on Sunday, perhaps attend a small group during the week, and try to have some spiritual disciplines in our lives. We may even engage in a mission project or respond to special appeals. But most of our life is lived elsewhere—in the so-called world. There is often little integration between our relationship with Jesus and life as we live it.

Yet the Kingdom demands the opposite. It is not identified by sacred spaces, places, times or even special people. The Kingdom is on the move because God is making His enemies His friends, reclaiming His good creation, and bringing this occupied planet under His Lordship. Jesus, as we have seen, was committed to extending God's kingdom throughout the land. He proclaimed the Kingdom's presence ("at hand" and "within reach"), delivered the demonized, and healed the sick. This was God's reign in action, overcoming the other reign in the world that held people in bondage.

N. T. Wright proposed that we could best understand Jesus' itinerant mission using the analogy of a political campaign.[1] Similar to a modern candidate for office, Jesus moved quickly from village to village, announcing the in-breaking of God's kingdom and setting people free. As He did so, He left behind cells of life, embracing those who had been touched by the King and who had experienced the Kingdom. Many people joined the multitudes that were seeking Jesus out, listening to His teaching and receiving His healing. They returned home transformed and told others of what the Lord had done for them (see Mark 5:19). They now belonged to the New Israel, and one day they would share in a fellowship baptized by the Spirit and would be sent forth to tell the nations of the world the good news of Christ.

Just as John Wesley traveled throughout England in the eighteenth century and left renewed fellowships within the established Church, so Jesus traveled throughout Galilee and left renewed fellowships within the synagogues. He covered as much ground as possible and taught His disciples by having them watch what He did and follow His example. Jesus' mission had two thrusts: building Kingdom communities and training His followers to extend the Kingdom.

Like many other Christians, when I was formally trained for ministry, I was equipped for church maintenance rather than church growth. Building networks of Kingdom communities was a foreign concept to me. The model was to graduate from theological seminary, join a church staff (probably doing youth work), gain experience over a few years, and then climb the ecclesiastical ladder to a pulpit position. Later, when the Jesus Movement hit in the late 1960s, I knew that I needed a new model. When I later met John Wimber, leader of the Vineyard Movement, I knew that I had found it. John helped me to take a fresh look at Jesus and His kingdom. Here is what I learned.

JESUS' MODEL

All Christians agree that Jesus came to set us free. Usually, this is defined as freedom from the penalty of sin through His death on the cross and freedom from the power of death through His resurrection.

Most would also affirm that Jesus has delivered us from Satan, even if this is often only a formality. But to see Jesus as one who liberates us from the oppressive powers and structures that hold us in legalism, idolatry, poverty, racism and addiction or who liberates us from the forces that exploit cheap labor and irreplaceable natural resources in this world pushes us beyond traditional evangelicalism.

Some brand those who advocate these ideas as "liberals," with all the negative theological and political implications connected with that term. Historically, this is not the case. The great revivalists, such as John Wesley in the eighteenth century and Charles Finney in the nineteenth century, along with politicians such as William Wilberforce in England, were leaders in social change. Evangelicals educated the poor, championed the end of slavery, built the temperance movement and provided social resources for immigrants moving into the industrialized urban areas.

Nevertheless, today it is common to hear that Jesus only cares about our souls: "Get saved and go to heaven." The disintegration of our planet is often viewed as the fulfillment of prophecy leading up to the events of the end times. But let's get a new biblical perspective and see what it really means to be a Christ follower.

A Background Reminder

When Satan revolted in heaven, he led a hierarchy of angels to join him. From that time on, they functioned as dark superpower spirits over territories and as low-level demons that afflicted individuals. While the Old Testament makes some reference to this, this fact becomes clear in the New Testament.

The apostle Paul, for example, had a warfare worldview. In 2 Corinthians 2:11, he warned Christians to be on guard against the devil's schemes. He stated that dark powers were behind the political and religious leaders who "crucified the Lord of glory" (1 Cor. 2:6-8) and used the Law of God to hold them in bondage. But Christ came to break their hold and lift the Law's indictment from them:

> When you were dead in your sins and in the uncircumcision of your sinful nature, God made you alive with Christ. He forgave us all our sins, having canceled the written code, with its regulations, that was against us and that stood opposed to us; he took it away, nailing it to the cross. And having disarmed the powers and authorities, he made public spectacle of them, triumphing over them by the cross (Col. 2:13-15).

Paul adds that while these powers and authorities could no longer beat them up under the Law, if they went back under it and embraced legalistic religion, they would be enslaved all over again by "the elemental spirits of the universe" (Gal. 4:8-9, *RSV*). In Christ however, they were secure in God's love and protected from such bondage:

> For I am convinced that neither death nor life, neither angels nor demons, neither the present nor the future, nor any powers, neither height nor depth, no anything else in all creation, will be able to separate us from the love of God that is in Christ Jesus our Lord (Rom. 8:38-39).

In sum, because Jesus is the Warrior King, bringing the Kingdom to us, He liberates us from Satan's kingdom and the idolatrous political, religious and legal structures that hold us in bondage. Jesus doesn't simply save souls. He creates a new order—a new community, a new Israel—where mercy and justice reign, and extends it into every area of society.

The New Temple

To understand how radical Jesus was, we must read the Gospels in the context of first-century Judaism. N. T. Wright has suggested that the Temple was the incarnational symbol of Judaism.[2] The rabbis called Jerusalem the navel of the universe, and at the center of that navel was the Jewish Temple. It was God's palace where heaven and Earth met. His presence dwelt in the inner shrine, the Holy of Holies, and He was only approachable through blood offered on the altar.

The Temple itself was immense and spectacular. The platform of the Temple, equivalent to 26 football fields in size, took up a quarter of the city. Josephus, the Jewish historian, reported that its inner shrine was gold-plated. When the sun rose over the Judean hills, onlookers were blinded by its glory. The Temple determined much of Jewish life: daily prayers and sacrifices, festivals, decisions about what was clean or unclean, and who was in the community and who was considered out of it (see Lev. 11–15).

Various feasts and festivals were celebrated at the Temple, including Yom Kippur, the Day of Atonement, and Passover, a central feast that celebrated Israel's deliverance from Egypt. The Temple was also the focal point of much wealth (with all the accompanying corruption). The priests amassed a huge treasury through annual taxes, tithes, offerings, bequests, money changing and the sale of sacrificial animals.

But Jesus came to replace the Temple. He dismantled Israel's central identity marker and re-established it in Himself. Now, instead of having to go to the Temple for forgiveness, people could obtain forgiveness directly through Christ. As N. T. Wright states, Jesus launched a "counter-Temple movement."[3]

The Gospel of Mark paints the picture. In Mark 2, Jesus was back in Capernaum teaching at home. The people heard that

He had returned, and soon crowds filled and spilled outside of the house where He was. As Jesus was teaching, four men arrived carrying a paralyzed friend. Because it was impossible for them to get to Jesus, they decided to climb a staircase to the roof, dig through its clay and timbers, create an opening, and lower the man down.

Jesus responded in a surprising way. He said to the paralytic, "Your sins are forgiven." The religious leaders reacted critically to this statement, because they knew that only God can forgive sins. (They think, *Blasphemy*.) Jesus knew this in His spirit, challenged them, and commanded the paralytic to take up his bed and walk. Jesus then said, "Why are you thinking these things? Which is easier: to say to the paralytic, 'Your sins are forgiven,' or to say, 'Get up, take your mat and walk'? But that you may know that the Son of Man has authority on earth to forgive sins" (Mark 2:8-10). Jesus then healed the paralytic. As the man walked out, everyone was amazed and praised God.

Here we see that Jesus liberated us from the Temple's religious and sacrificial system. He usurped its function, moving forgiveness from that place to His person. In doing so, He did what only God could do. The event of forgiveness was displayed as the paralytic was healed. His gift from Jesus was forgiveness and healing.

God's forgiveness was now in Jesus, the Son of God. The whole religious system, in Israel, corrupted and politicized, would be destroyed within a generation. Jesus was the Son of Man (exalted Messianic figure) who had authority on Earth, right now, in that place to forgive sins.

While the Church has tried to move forgiveness back into sacred places under the control of sacred people, Jesus overturns that system. To be a Christ follower, then, is to set people free from impersonal rituals of forgiveness or repetitively sacrificing Christ on the altar.[4] Forgiveness is in the person of Christ, based on His perfect once-for-all death for sin on the cross.

Jesus still forgives and liberates people today. I remember a teenager named Cheryl, who found her way into Hollywood First Presbyterian Church one Sunday. She had lived as a hippie on the Sunset Strip for several years and was now pregnant. Having been with so many men, she had no clue as to the identity of her unborn child's father. In desperation, she came to church—the largest one in Hollywood, so that she would be lost in the crowd.

But as I preached, God touched her. She waited for me at the door, mascara running down her cheeks. We sat down in the empty sanctuary as she poured out her heart. When she said that she was too sinful for God to accept her, I knew that she was not far from the Kingdom. I shared with her that Jesus was with her, had died for her sins and was ready to forgive her. She could begin a new life. I remember reciting 1 John 1:9 to her: "If we confess our sins, he is faithful and just to forgive us our sins and cleanse us from all unrighteousness."

Within 20 minutes, it was all over (or it had just begun). Cheryl opened her heart to Jesus. Like the paralytic, Cheryl "took up her bed and walked." She then dealt with the paralysis of her pregnancy by deciding to have her baby but give it up for adoption. We arranged for her to have a bed in a Salvation Army home for unwed mothers. Since this was back in the 1960s, when her baby was born, she saw him for a moment, and then he was gone.

Like the paralytic, Cheryl was forgiven and free. She was free from the guilt and shame that would have come from destroying this little life. She was free from the sexual pain of her past. She became a key player as we jumped into the Jesus Movement. She took me to the streets of Hollywood and was a change agent for our seeing thousands come to Christ.

There is a postscript to this story. Eighteen years later, while I was living in San Diego, Cheryl called. Her baby, now grown, had found her. He had been adopted by a family in Seattle and had become a Christian. Now, Cheryl told me through her tears, he was moving south that summer to live with her. This is the power of Jesus who said to the paralytic, "Son, your sins are forgiven" and then commanded him, "Take up your bed and walk."

A New Holiness

Along with the Temple service, the Israelites were called to be a holy people, mirroring God's holiness. This translated into every area of Jewish life, starting with male circumcision. A whole range of laws separated Israel's daily life from all that was considered profane or unclean. This, of course, included the Gentiles with their pagan gods and goddesses and their corrupt lives. Holiness intentionally isolated Israel from the nations. The Jews lived a separated life, even in the midst of pagan groups. Like the Temple, this too was a central marker to their identity. But Jesus not only liberated them from dead ritual, He also liberated them from religious, self-protecting communities.

For the Jews, the issue was being holy as God was holy. To be His holy people, lines had to be drawn, racial purity had to be enforced, and the Law had to be rigorously applied. Israel, at its core, was exclusive, but Jesus shattered this. Rather than being exclusive, He was inclusive. In Mark 2:14, He called a hated tax collector—a collaborator with Rome—into His inner circle and then ate with him and his "sinner" friends. Mark tells us that they formed a sizable crowd.

The religious leaders were offended. How could Jesus follow the holy God yet fellowship with unholy people? Jesus' response was that it is not the healthy who need a doctor, but the sick (see v. 17). Those who think they are healthy don't need Jesus. But the sick need a doctor, and Jesus had come for them (and you and me). He told the religious leaders, "I have not come to call the righteous, but sinners" (v. 17).

We must ask ourselves, *Would we want Jesus to move into our neighborhood? Who would He bring with Him? What would happen to our property values? Would we want the people Jesus hangs with to date our daughter?* Jesus violated every rule of ritual purity and social acceptability. His behavior provoked a spiritual crisis when He forgave sins and a social crisis when He ate with sinners. But the walls had to come down. Jesus had come to break through the religious, social, economic and political structures that separated people from each other and perpetuated the brokenness of this world. Jesus had come to heal people and reconcile them to the Father and to each other.

Years ago, as a college sophomore at Princeton University, I was invited to attend a midweek meeting of the Rock Church in New York City. This was my first experience in a Pentecostal service, and I was extremely uncomfortable and critical. The music was led by the pastor's wife, who reminded me of a cheerleader at a football game. Then a couple of people were called forward to have demons cast out of them (having had no context for this, I was offended at the time). Next, the pastor preached a sermon from the book of Revelation denouncing intellectualism. It seemed so mindless to me.

I say all of this to make my point: Although I was uncomfortable during the service, I couldn't help but notice that among the several hundred people present, there were many African-Americans, working men in trade uniforms, maids and secretaries, along with some socialites dressed in furs, looking like they just stepped out of a Fifth Avenue showroom. I had never seen such a mixed crowd. Then, after the service, while the majority of the congregation lingered, I saw a well-dressed white woman hug a black waitresses in a uniform.

This was occurring all over the congregation. There was an explosion of love, with people embracing each other, praying for each other, and weeping with each other. The racial mix was startling—this was in 1956, way before the Civil Rights movement had gained momentum. My lasting impression was that this church was an inclusive community in the heart of the city. Despite the cultural and theological issues I encountered, redemption and reconciliation were real to me that night—the clear fruit of the gospel.

Years later, I visited a Mexican-American man in prison, whom I will call Juan. Gang tattoos covered his arms and chest. While serving time for shooting a couple of people in a convenience store robbery in Texas, he came to Christ and began to correspond with a woman involved in prison ministry. They fell in love and asked me to perform their wedding on the day of his release, which I did.

Juan had a sweet heart, and Jesus was changing his life. After the wedding, the couple took off for a week and then came to church. One of our leaders, not having a clue as to who Juan was, asked him to help take the offering. I will never forget seeing Juan walk down the aisle to do his job. I thought to myself, *What would people think if they knew that a Mexican gang member—a murderer and an ex-con—was passing the collection plates?*

This is the inclusive, transforming community that Jesus came to build. Church gets interesting when it is socially and culturally diverse, when we can't figure out why these people are together. Then it dawns on us—it must be Jesus.

A New Piety

For the Israelites, holiness was expressed in pious acts, such as fasting. The Jews kept fasting days as a sign of repentance, mourning and sorrow for their sin. Fasting in Jesus' time was especially relevant, because the Romans were occupying the Promised Land. In fasting, Israel cried out for deliverance.

However, in Mark 2:18, Jesus liberated His followers from imposed spiritual disciplines as markers of their piety. John the Baptist's disciples fasted, and the disciples of the Pharisees (religious leaders) fasted, but Jesus' disciples did not. When people came to Jesus and asked Him why this was so, Jesus responded that in this Kingdom-come time, fasting was inappropriate. His presence was not meant to be a funeral; it was to be a wedding. "How can the guests of the bridegroom fast while he is with them?" He asked (v. 19). Weddings are for celebration, and in the ancient Jewish culture, they went on for days.

Jesus was replacing fasting with feasting. The demonized were being delivered, the sick were being healed, and the good news was being preached to the poor. Jesus was like the bridegroom at a wedding celebration, and His disciples were like the attendants (see v. 19). So long as the bridegroom was present, how could they fast?

The old forms of piety were out. Jesus told those who had questioned Him that no one would sew a patch of unshrunk cloth on old clothes, for when the clothes are washed, they would tear (see v. 21). In the same way, no one would pour new wine into old wineskins, for when it fermented, it would crack (see v. 22). No, this was party time. New forms, new skins, must express the new age, the Kingdom age now upon them.

Yet there was a caveat here: This magic moment would pass and turn to sorrow. There is an appropriate time to experience repentance, loss and grief—in classical language, "to mortify the flesh." The Kingdom had come, but it was not fully come. A time would come when the bridegroom would be taken from the disciples, and then they would fast. For the first time, the shadow of the cross loomed over Jesus. But that darkness could not subvert the light that had come into the world.

The concept of this being "party time" hit home for me during the height of the Jesus Movement when a man named Verne came to our crash pad where we took people off the streets. Verne's assets were his beautiful tenor voice, winsome personality and command of his guitar. His father was a bishop in the Mormon Church in Colorado. Verne had grown up in a very controlled family. He had rebelled, become heavily involved in the sex, drugs and rock 'n' roll scene, and then hit the streets.

Running from the law, Verne was picked up by a van coming down the California coast. He joined several other people in the back, who were passing around a joint. However, when the joint came to a longhaired person seated beside Verne, the man simply said, "No thanks, I'm a Christian" and passed it on. When the van arrived in Los Angeles, this Christian invited Verne to come with him to our house.

The two showed up late that afternoon, with Verne, slightly stoned, carrying a knapsack and a guitar. At about that time, the housemates decided to have a Bible study from John 3, which speaks about being "born again." When I later joined the group, they had just wrapped up and everyone was shouting, "Verne has just accepted the Lord!" I welcomed Verne into the Kingdom, and as I looked into his smiling eyes, I saw that they were clear. It was as if a light had come on.

That night, Verne was in our coffee house, The Salt Company, making up songs about Jesus. His family life and his Mormonism had included enforced fasting, but now it was party time. Verne would become one of the key evangelists in the Jesus Movement, bringing thousands to Christ through his incredible voice and compelling testimony.

A New Sabbath

Keeping the Sabbath law was a central Jewish marker. Just as God created the world in six days, the Israelites were to work for six days. Just as God rested on the seventh day, the Israelites were to rest on the seventh day. The Israelites were to imitate the God they worshiped in the structure of their lives.

The Sabbath was so central to Jewish law that keeping it appeared in the Ten Commandments. To violate the Sabbath was to violate God's calling for His people to be holy as He was holy. A vast legal tradition soon grew up guarding the Sabbath. People were forbidden from lighting a fire on the Sabbath, for that was considered work. They couldn't thread a needle; that was considered work. They were commanded to rest from everything that could be considered work, just as God rests.

In Mark 2:23, the religious leaders again criticized Jesus for allowing His hungry disciples to pick grain on the Sabbath. After arguing for precedent from David, Jesus pushed on, stating that one greater than David had arrived: "The Son of Man is Lord even of the Sabbath" (v. 28).

Along with everything else, Jesus liberated us from the Sabbath law. He freed us from religious performance based on legalism. Jesus ripped away all the religious and legal prescriptions around the Sabbath and simply announced that we were not made for the Sabbath, the Sabbath was made for us. So, if we are hungry, we should get food. If we are diseased, we should get healed. God is not resting on the Sabbath (see John 5:17). He is working for us, providing for us, healing us. God reveals Himself in Jesus and gives Him sovereign authority over the Sabbath. If we look to Jesus, we will learn how to keep the Sabbath. It is made to bless us. It is God's gift to us. We are now free from the burdensome nitpicking on how to define our Sabbath rest.

When I started at Princeton University, I found a rigorous Christian group on campus led by a Bible teacher who had graduated there years ago. He insisted on strict separation from the world. He prohibited all movies. Before the Junior Prom, he asked us how we would feel if Jesus returned while we were "whirling around the dance floor." The legalism was intense, and we were constantly warned against false teachers.

As a result, my roommate refused to set foot on the Seminary campus two blocks away, lest he "compromise his testimony." Our dominant motive became the fear of God's rejection and the fear of the rejection from our leader. Shame was covered by wooden obedience. We read only the *King James Version* of the Bible and witnessed door to door in the dorms, telling our classmates that they were going to hell.

I lived in this straight jacket for a year, finding my identity and security there. I was exemplary, outdoing most of the rest, deeply fearful, gaining position with performance for acceptance. Yet when I decided to major in religion ("sit under false teachers"), I was ostracized by the group. Like many of the first-century Jews, I was told that I was made for strict obedience to the Law and all its fine points of interpretation.

Once I escaped this group's control, my joy and freedom returned. I realized that I wasn't made for the Sabbath; the Sabbath was made for me. I realized that the truth of the gospel stood up to the most critical and rigorous examination, and I didn't have to be afraid to study and think. I realized that Jesus, the Son of Man, was the Lord of all "religious" activities. He was Lord of the Sabbath. (And remember—He had fun on the Sabbath!)

SUMMING IT UP

Jesus is our Liberator. He liberates us from demonic powers that use sacred spaces, rituals and people. Forgiveness is His work and His gift. He liberates us from restrictive, exclusive fellowships. His arms are outstretched to welcome all—especially sinners—to His table. He liberates us from religious disciplines that display our piety rather than expose our hearts. He turns our sorrow into celebration. He liberates us from performing for God so that we can be like God, fulfilling His intention for the Sabbath.

In other words, Jesus is intensely political. He liberates us from a whole vision, culture and style of what it means to be God's people in this world. He is our forgiveness, our welcome, our celebration and our freedom. As the Son of Man, He has authority on Earth to forgive sins and heal sinners. He is the good physician who comes for the sick. He is the bridegroom, hosting the wedding. He is Lord of the Sabbath. And He recreates us to be a community of forgiveness, openness, celebration and freedom. We then move from religion to relationship and from sacred places to the sacred Person, who welcomes tax collectors and sinners like us.

Enter the Kingdom through the gate marked "All Things New." This is gospel indeed!

CHAPTER 11

KINGDOM SURPRISES

Rick Whitehill, psychologist and professor at the University of California, San Diego, was a convert from Judaism who joined our church. As we chatted one day, he commented, "When I came to Christ, I gave up the illusion of control." I thought, *That's it.* We all desperately want to be in control. We demand that Jesus fit our perception of reality or worldview. We expect Him to answer our prayers in our way by our timetable, and we become angry if He doesn't. We want an orderly faith congruent with our longing for an orderly life. But Jesus never fits our mold. We can't capture or domesticate Him.

As Jesus announced the in-breaking of God's kingdom in Himself, He turned Jewish Messianic expectations on their head. As we have seen, Jesus trained His followers to extend His ministry: "He appointed twelve—designating them apostles—that they might be with him and that he might send them out to preach [the Kingdom] and to have authority to drive out demons." (Mark 3:14-15). For the Jews, "12" is a magic number. Jacob's 12 sons formed Israel's 12 tribes in the first Exodus from Pharaoh's kingdom. By selecting 12 apostles, Jesus reconstituted Israel for the final Exodus. His mighty works and symbolic acts filled the air with wild hopes. As Moses delivered

God's people from Egypt, Jesus would now deliver them from Rome. Indeed, He recapitulated Israel's history in Himself, but then twisted it in a whole new direction and gave it a whole new meaning.

No wonder the in-breaking of the Kingdom raised bewildered responses: "The people were all so amazed that they asked each other, 'What is this? A new teaching—and with authority! He even gives orders to evil spirits and they obey him'" (Mark 1:27). "Why does this fellow talk like that? He's blaspheming! Who can forgive sins but God alone?" (2:7). "This amazed everyone and they praised God, saying, 'We have never seen anything like this!'" (2:12).

Some knew that God was in their midst, and they worshiped Christ (see Mark 2:12). Some concluded that Jesus was crazy: "When his family heard about this, they went to take charge of him, for they said, 'He is out of his mind'" (3:21). Still others charged that He was demon-possessed: "And the teachers of the law who came down from Jerusalem said, 'He is possessed by Beelzebub [Lord of Filth]! By the prince of demons he is driving out demons'" (v. 22). Jesus used sheer logic to refute this last accusation that He was in league with the devil by saying, "How can Satan drive out Satan? If a kingdom is divided against itself, that kingdom cannot stand" (v. 23). Jesus was saying that if He had sided with Satan, He would be driving demons *into* people, not *out of* people. The devil would never make a pact with Jesus to assault his own kingdom and set captives free. The devil isn't that dumb. Instead, Jesus had come to tie up Satan, the strong man, and plunder his possessions (see v. 27).

PARABLES OF THE KINGDOM

Like any good rabbi, Jesus taught through His works every bit as much as through His words. His mighty acts formed the platform for His parables of the Kingdom, which He next delivered to the crowds in Mark 4 from the safety of an offshore boat. Today, the Church has it backward—we think people should be drawn to our words. But Jesus thought that people should be drawn to our works: "You are the light of the world. A city on a hill cannot be hidden. In the same way, let your light shine before men [and women], that they may see your good deeds and praise your Father in heaven" (Matt. 5:14-16). Obviously, Jesus was not only taking about healing people and casting out demons. He was referring to the whole range of good works that display the power, compassion and justice of God.

I remember once meeting two young Vineyard pastors from Belfast who decided to do something for the Kingdom instead of merely speaking about it. So they took a chair, put it in on a busy street, and invited sick people to sit in it while they prayed for their healing. More than 50 percent of the people the pastors prayed for were healed on the spot. Don't simply write this off as the luck of the Irish. The pastors stepped out in faith, and the Kingdom showed up.

So, as Jesus taught on the Sea of Galilee's shore, He told stories, or parables—pictures with punch. These stories were all about the kingdom of God. Remember the expectations of the first-century Jews: When the Kingdom arrived, Rome would be expelled, idols would be destroyed, the land would be cleansed, and Israel would be restored and vindicated in all her glory. But Jesus painted a different picture. What were His basic themes, and how can they help us understand Kingdom ministry today?

Kingdom Conflict

Using the Parable of the Sower (see Mark 4:1-25), Jesus taught that we live in the age in which God's kingdom is both fruitful and assaulted. It is like a farmer who first sowed his seed on unprepared soil and then plowed it in (exactly the way land was farmed in Galilee).[1] His sowing was extravagant—he threw seed everywhere.

Some of the seed landed on the path, some on the shallow soil, some among thorns, and some on good and receptive soil.

The harvest depended on the soil on which the seed landed. Seed that fell on the path was devoured by birds. Seed that fell on shallow soil sprouted, but then was scorched by the sun. Seed that fell among thorns was choked. But the seed that fell on good soil yielded a rich harvest. N. T. Wright suggests that this is a picture of Israel. She is like the seed. Her history is a mixed bag of opposition and failure, but with Jesus, in the final Exodus, a gigantic harvest is coming. She will be fruitful at last.[2]

More specifically, Jesus depicted Himself as the one sowing the seed of the Kingdom. But His success (and that of His followers) would be mixed: The birds (representing the devil) would gobble up some of the exposed seed and steal it before the message took root. The seed that sprouted in shallow soil would be scorched by the sun (symbolizing the persecution of the Early Church), and many who responded to the Kingdom would fall away the minute they were attacked or challenged. The seed that fell in the thorns would be choked by the cares and riches of this world—many would find their loyalty to Jesus throttled when the world system moved in again and seduced them. But Jesus told them not to get discouraged. The harvest would come from the good seed that fell on good soil. This harvest is still coming in today, and it is gigantic.

This parable describes the mixed reception that Jesus and His followers would receive. In the same way, because we minister in the tension of the Kingdom come and coming, there is no triumph here. Opposition is everywhere: from Satan, from persecution, and from the worries of this life. Jesus may be popular today and crucified tomorrow. As it was for Him, so it is with us.

Again and again, I have seen people profess Christ and spring to life. I think of one movie producer I knew whose Jewish father committed suicide when he was young, leaving a deep ache inside his heart. A friend finally brought him to a Sunday church service. He wept through it, prayed to receive Christ, and went back to his office the next day to tell his staff that he had become a Christian. But he proved to be like the seed that fell on thorny soil. The cares of this world began to choke him. A lovely Muslim woman came into his life, and other events occurred to make him question God. His faith had no depth. He withered away, and I carry sorrow for him to this day.

Jesus was more realistic than most Christians. We are locked in battle. Many fall, and we weep for them. But we must take heart, knowing that a great harvest is on the way. One sign of that harvest occurred when the Jesus Movement hit in the late 1960s. At the time, the Unites States was coming unglued. Race riots exploded in our nation's inner cities. Ghettos burned. Campuses went on strike and shut down. The drug culture bloomed and the pill allowed people to have sex without any apparent consequences. Through folk music and rock 'n' roll, youth editorialized to youth. The Vietnam War ground on. Draft cards burned and deserters fled to Canada. John Kennedy was shot down; then Martin Luther King, Jr.; and then Bobby Kennedy. It seemed that the nation was headed for civil war. Yet in the midst of all this chaos, something incredible happened.

On the West Coast, a new breed of Christians emerged in little pockets out of the counter culture, and the seed of the Kingdom was thrown everywhere. These Christians hit the streets, held concerts in parks, witnessed on the beaches, and traveled up and down California in vans with "One Way" bumper stickers. Our Presbyterian church jumped in and opened a coffee house in Hollywood. Soon, our church's 2,000-seat sanctuary was filled on Friday nights as kids listened to "Jesus music" and heard their own evangelists preach. Waves of revival broke across the nation. Churches, such as

Calvary Chapel, mushroomed. It was estimated that within a few years, three million new converts came into the Church. Out of conflict and discouragement, God brought a great harvest. Jesus promises us that more is to come.

Kingdom Crisis

Jesus taught that when the Kingdom comes, everything will be "smoked out" and revealed. Like a lamp put on a stand, the Kingdom will light the whole house (see Mark 4:21). The King and His kingdom precipitate the time when everything must come out of hiding. The pride, legalism and hypocrisy of religion will be revealed. All satanic powers, all heresy, all hidden agendas, all lies of the enemy, all perverse motives of people's hearts, all political alliances, all idols and addictions, all family pain, all insecurities and shame—all will be exposed. "For whatever is hidden is meant to be disclosed, and whatever is concealed is meant to be brought out into the open. If anyone has ears to hear, let him hear" (Mark 4:22-23).

In this final battle, Satan's designs and demons will be forced to manifest. They already know who Jesus is, as Mark states: "He [Jesus] also drove out many demons, but he would not let the demons speak because they knew who he was" (1:34). The evil one will be exposed, and we will be exposed. This will be the crisis hour that anticipates the final Day of Judgment.

During the Jesus Movement, the entire Hollywood scene was before us: pimps, prostitutes, witches, runaways, dealers, druggies, gangsters, lost souls getting more lost in Tinsel Town. However, much of this was hidden and concealed, like a movie set, behind Hollywood's false fronts. But our presence on the streets offered an alternative. Light shines in the darkness. A band of young people loving Jesus and loving each other cut through much of the hypocrisy, crime and sheer evil. The truth of the gospel exposed the lies of the enemy.

One night, I was invited to a Nichiren Shoshu Buddhist meeting in a Hollywood home. After rousing singing, 50 or so of us listened to a young evangelist preach their "gospel." He promised that if we would learn to chant, we would align ourselves with the force of the universe. As a result, we would get anything we wanted. "Chant for a job, and you will get a job," he said. "Chant for a car, and you will get a car. Chant for a girl, and you will get a girl."

After the presentation, the speaker called for questions. I raised my hand. "If I were dying of cancer, what would you say to me?" He avoided responding and went on, "Chant for a car, and you will get a car." I raised my hand again.

"You didn't answer my question. If I were dying, what would you say to me?" He replied, "We aren't into death; we're into life. Anyway, no one has come back from the dead to tell us."

I couldn't hold back. "You're wrong," I said. "Someone has come back from the dead. Jesus Christ is risen and He has told us." With that, the group leader closed the meeting, and I was quickly ushered out: "Whatever is hidden is meant to be disclosed, and whatever is concealed is meant to be brought out into the open. If anyone has ears to hear, let him hear" (Mark 4:22).

Kingdom Generosity

Jesus said that we are responsible for responding to the message of the Kingdom: "Consider carefully what you hear" (Mark 4:24). Like a person at a market buying grain, "with the measure you use, it will be measured to you" (v. 24). But God is generous. Jesus said that we would get even more than we could hold: "Whoever has will be given more" (v. 25). However, if we reject the Kingdom, we face a total wipeout. This is the force of "whoever does not have, even what he has will be taken from him" (v. 25). But how can we have something taken away when we don't have it in the first place?

While this doesn't seem to make sense, we need to remember that the Kingdom has broken in on us. This is the crisis hour, and judgment and redemption are here. No one gets off. But those who respond to the King and enter the Kingdom receive more and more of God's generosity.

Again and again, God has surprised me. He surprised me by calling me into His kingdom when I was in high school. He surprised me when He called me to one of the dynamic student ministries in the nation. He surprised me when He threw me into the Jesus Movement. He surprised me when He gave me Kathryn, my wonderful wife. He surprised me when He filled me with His Spirit, opening me up to a whole new world. He surprised me when He moved me into a dying church to spark revival. He surprised me when He showed me that the sick can be healed and the oppressed can be delivered. He surprised me when He had me fired from my former church and then called me into the Vineyard to plant a new church. He has surprised me with an incredible spiritual family across the world. And He continues to surprise me again and again with prophetic direction for my future.

Kingdom Ministry

Jesus also taught that there is a mystery about the Kingdom. It is like the farmer who scatters seed. Night and day, the seed sprouts and grows, although the farmer "does not know how" (Mark 4:27). It is the soil that is producing fruit, in stages: "All by itself, the soil produces grain—first the stalk, then the head, then the full kernel in the head" (v. 28). But there is mystery here, because we are not in control of the Kingdom's growth. This is God's work. When the grain is fully ripe, it's harvest time. This is a common metaphor for the final in-gathering. Jesus is now scattering the seed that is mysteriously growing. Don't expect the end of the age to come before the harvest is ready.

It is important for us not to confuse the Church with the Kingdom. The Church is an instrument of God's reign breaking in upon us, but it is not that reign. We can measure the Church. We can learn principles of church growth. We can see churches come and go, ministries rise and fall, waves of revival break and pass. Church history is always a mixed bag. We need to study it critically and repent for our sins and failures. But in the midst of all of this, Jesus promises that the Kingdom is growing.

In our own lives, Kingdom seed may lie dormant for years. A young man I knew, named Timothy, grew up in a church-going family that was ripped apart by divorce. He spent many years medicating his pain with alcohol, drugs, sex and dangerous street life. At one point, he had an emotional breakdown. But his mother, who was a serious believer, continued to pray for him.

One summer, some friends brought Timothy to a Soul Survivor youth festival held in the English countryside. Timothy refused to enter into the worship, but he listened to the messages. Finally, on the last afternoon of the festival, Timothy and I sat together behind a huge circus tent that held 10,000 kids. He was ready to pepper me with his objections to Christianity. But God had other things in mind. We had no sooner sat down than Timothy began to open up his heart to me. All the past pain came tumbling out. I just listened. Finally, I simply asked him if he wanted to ask Jesus into his heart. We prayed, and the seed—sown long ago and nurtured through his mother's prayers—sprouted. Today, Timothy is married to a Christian woman and lives in the United States, building a Kingdom website and working in media.

As we share the good news of the Kingdom, we never know how the seed will grow and when the fruit will come. This is God's time. He is in control; we're not.

Kingdom Values

Jesus concluded by teaching that the kingdom of God is like the smallest seed imaginable (see Mark 4:31). It looks so little and foolish. But this small seed grows. It will become the "largest of all garden plants, with such big branches that the birds of the air [a metaphor for the Gentile nations?] can perch in its shade." This Kingdom grows from small to large in our hearts and in our history. As it turns our worldly values upside down, the Kingdom will dominate God's garden and be a refuge for all peoples.

THE MYSTERY OF THE KINGDOM

It is important to note that while Jesus spoke these parables openly, their understanding was limited to His disciples, those on the inside. The Kingdom was revealed to them but concealed from others. These stories were signs of judgment, fulfilling Isaiah's heavy call: "They may be ever seeing but never perceiving, and ever hearing but never understanding, otherwise they might turn and be forgiven" (Mark 4:12; see also Isaiah 6:9). This is the paradox of the parables of the Kingdom: Jesus was no rabbi merely instructing people in the ways of God; He was the Messiah and Prophet of the Kingdom. He came with good news: The rule and reign of God are within reach.

This is not open for complaint, critique or conversation. We are in the crisis hour and we must respond: This is the only way inside—the only way to become a Christ follower. Otherwise, we are on the outside and will never understand Jesus or His stories. However, when we repent and believe, Jesus then teaches us the meaning of His stories. Our value system, demanding a Davidic Conqueror driving Rome into the sea, is replaced by the true Davidic King who sets the demonized free, heals the sick, and begins to restore this fallen creation.

Jesus' Kingdom teachings centered around seed, light and harvest. They revealed extravagant waste, violent opposition, and expectations turned upside down. The smallest seed would grow into the greatest tree, but how this would occur was a mystery. The clue lies in the Cross. This takes us to the subject of Kingdom suffering as we journey with Jesus.

CHAPTER 12

THE ROAD MARKED "SUFFERING"

One question that is often asked is, If God is all powerful and all good, why is there meaningless suffering in our world? Suffering is a theme that we all prefer to avoid in favor of a "good time" gospel. Surely, we reason, we have had enough! Our lives are so broken. But we must follow the real Jesus, who offers no cheap psychological fixes. As we have seen, His role is paradoxical: He is both the triumphant Davidic Warrior-King and the humiliated Suffering Servant of the Lord. So how do we put these two roles together—the crown and the cross—and what difference does it make for our lives?

Throughout the first eight chapters of Mark's Gospel, Jesus revealed His "power ministry," manifesting the reign and rule of God in people's midst. In Mark 4, He calmed a raging storm. In Mark 5 and 6, He drove out a legion of demons, raised a little girl from the dead, and fed a hungry multitude by multiplying a little boy's lunch. The crowds flocked around Him. The circle of Christ followers grew. All of this was dramatic, even cataclysmic.

In contrast to Jesus' Kingdom power, however, there was Jesus' Kingdom suffering. The more success Jesus had, the more opposition He faced. His enemies knew that their whole religious-political system was under threat. The clues leading to the cross appear.

The first half of the Gospel of Mark climaxes with Jesus drawing His disciples aside into Gentile territory, where they can be alone. On the way, He asks them a general question: "Who do people say I am?" (8:27). They offer multiple answers: John the Baptist, Elijah, one of the prophets. But Jesus' general question is always for the sake of His specific question: "But what about you? Who do you say that I am?" (v. 29). Peter responds, "You are the Christ [You are the anointed of God; You are the Messianic King; You are the final David to come]" (v. 29).

While Jesus accepts Peter's confession, He orders His disciples not to tell anyone about Him. He breaks the Messianic mold and pours radically new content into it. Rather than marching on Jerusalem with swords gleaming and blood flowing, Jesus marches on Jerusalem where His blood will flow: "He then began to teach them that the Son of Man [exalted Messianic figure] must suffer many things and be rejected by the elders, chief priests and teachers of the law, and that he must be killed and after three days rise again" (v. 31). Wanting the best for Jesus, Peter rebukes Him (see v. 32). Jesus returns the favor, seeing the dark shadow of Satan behind Peter's goodwill that is tempting Him away from the cross. The same enemy who met Jesus in the wilderness (see 1:12) raises his ugly head again.

PASSION PREDICTIONS

Then in Mark 8:31-32, Jesus gives the first of three passion predictions, which will punctuate chapters 8 to 10 of Mark. When we compare this first prediction to the others found in Mark 9:31 and 10:33-34, we find that the last two lack the phrase, "the Son of Man must suffer many things." It was dropped because at that time it was already being fulfilled. Suffering marked His whole ministry, but now Jesus would go intentionally to Jerusalem to die. Paradoxically, this is how He will reign from the cross: "King of the Jews." Let's briefly trace this theme of suffering to determine the levels of suffering that Jesus endured and what this means for us as Christ followers.

Suffering, Level One: Misunderstood by Family

First, Jesus suffers the misunderstanding and rejection of His family. While most of His family members later come to faith in Him, they don't start there (with the exception of His mother). As we have seen, they thought that He was crazy and wanted to restrain Him.

For the Jews, the legitimate son reflected the faith, morals and culture of his family. His parents defined his identity and vocation. They arranged his marriage and determined his destiny. He was raised to receive and pass on their world to the next generation. When Jesus challenged all of this, He suffered His family's rejection. In the same way, He warned His followers that if they surrendered their controlling family identity and embraced their new identity in Him, then they, too, would suffer. Listen to His hard words:

Do you think I came to bring peace on earth? No, I tell you, but division. From now on there will be five in one family divided against each other, three against two and two against three. They will be divided, father against son, and son against father, mother against daughter and daughter against mother, mother-in-law against daughter-in-law and daughter-in-law against mother-in-law (Luke 12:51-53).

Brother will betray brother to death, and a father his child; children will rebel against their parents and have them put to death. All men will hate you because of me, but he who stands firm to the end will be saved (Matt. 10:21-22).

This provides the context for one of Jesus' deepest confrontations:

Large crowds were traveling with Jesus, and turning to them he said, "If anyone comes to me and does not hate his father and mother, his wife and children, his brothers and sisters— yes and even his own life—he cannot be my disciple. And anyone who does not carry his cross and follow me [to death] cannot be my disciple" (Luke 14:25-27).

Some water this down and say that what Jesus really meant is that we are to love Him so much that our love for family looks like hatred in comparison. But this is a fantasy. Jesus was not addressing the commandment to honor one's father and mother here. Rather, He was telling us that if, as in first-century Judaism, our family determines our identity and destiny, we should abhor this idol and follow Christ alone. But the real idol is our own life. When we surrender and die to ourselves, then and only then do we become Christ followers. Kingdom seed will have fallen on good soil, and a large crop will follow.

When I came home as a new, excited Christian, my parents didn't share my joy. At that time, my engineer father resisted my challenge to his view that the world was a closed system of cause and effect. For him, God made the world, stepped back from it and let it run on its own by natural law. My mother resisted my challenge to her liberalism. She saw Jesus as one noble spiritual leader among many. One of her favorite wall hangings was the equivalent of the Golden Rule from all major religions.

As a new Christian, I was told to not preach to my parents. Well, I did, and, of course, they were dismayed. How could their 15-year-old son tell them that they were probably going to hell? Clearly, I was expressing my teenage rebellion in Christian terms. But this was not the core of my conversion or my heart. I was finding my new identity in Christ, and it was costly. Eventually, I calmed down, and they let up. But I still experienced the very real separation that Jesus warned of and that we still must hear:

> Whoever acknowledges me before men, I will also acknowledge him before my Father in heaven. But whoever disowns me before men, I will disown him before my Father in heaven. Do not suppose that I have come to bring peace, but a sword. For I have come to turn "a man against his father, a daughter against her mother, a daughter-in-law against her mother-in-law—a man's enemies will be the members of his own household." Anyone who loves his father or mother more than me is not worthy of me; anyone who loves his son or daughter more than me is not worthy of me; and anyone who does not take his cross and follow me is not worthy of me. Whoever finds his life will lose it and whoever loses his life for my sake will find it (Matt. 10:32-39).

Don't be surprised if your family doesn't immediately welcome your new faith. My failure was in mixing my adolescent rebellion with Jesus. It took time for the division to heal. Although my parents thought that I was just going through a phase, as I pressed on (and wised up) they softened. Then they became more and more supportive, even of my call to ministry. Some years later, my mother recommitted her life to Christ and recovered her childhood faith. Then, after my father retired, he attended a conference, sponsored by

Howard Butt, Jr., a lay evangelist from Texas. On a Saturday morning, as Howard gave the invitation, my father stood up and confessed Christ. Filled with joy, he was like a little boy all over again.

As new Christians, we must be committed to demonstration as well as proclamation. Our families need to see the difference that Jesus makes in our lives. But we must count the cost. Part of death to ourselves is death to securing our identity and destiny in our families, rather than in Jesus Himself. He alone is worthy of our worship. All idols will fall. So be warned: You will enter the Kingdom through the gate marked "Suffering."

Suffering, Level Two: Religious Resistance

In addition to family opposition, Jesus suffered persecution from this fallen world-system that is dominated by the devil. As we have seen, the Jewish religious leaders questioned Him, gathered opposition against Him, and planned His death. They knew that if Jesus got His way, their whole religious edifice would crumble. Indeed, His new wine would break their old wine skins.

As Jesus marched toward Jerusalem, the momentum built against Him: "The chief priests and the teachers of the law . . . began looking for a way to kill him, for they feared him, because the whole crowd was amazed at his teaching" (Mark 11:18). His "suffering many things" now included attacks against His authority (see vv. 27-33) and rejection by the religious leaders (see 12:1-12 in which Jesus evokes the Parable of the Vineyard, which symbolized Israel and its wicked tenants). Jesus' opponents tried to trap Him over such issues as paying taxes to Caesar (see 12:13-17), the doctrine of the resurrection (see vv. 18-27) and the Messiah being the son of David (see vv. 35-40).

In the midst of all this controversy, Jesus didn't back off. He charged the Pharisees with hypocrisy and pronounced judgment upon them. He told His disciples that these religious leaders said one thing but did another: "They do not practice what they preach" (23:3). They made a religious show for human approval, rather than divine approval: "Everything they do is done for men to see" (v. 5). They opposed Him, and in so doing, they opposed the Kingdom: "Woe to you, teachers of the law [scribes] and Pharisees, you hypocrites! You shut the kingdom of heaven in men's faces. You yourselves do not enter, nor will you let those enter who are trying to" (vv. 13-14). They tithed, but neglected the more important matters: "justice, mercy and faithfulness" (v. 23). They cleaned up their outer appearance, but left the inside corrupt: "On the outside you appear to people as righteous, but on the inside you are full of hypocrisy and wickedness" (v. 28). As descendents of those who killed the prophets, they would do the same to Jesus and His followers (vv. 33-34).

"Religion" will not let us off easily. Revival is always attacked by the establishment. When the Presbyterian Church I pastored in La Jolla, California, went into revival, the key elder arranged to have me fired. I confronted him on an ethical issue in his life and—to the shock and dismay of 1,000 members—rallied the other elders for a "palace revolution." The deeper issue behind this was the key elder's resistance to the freedom and power of the Holy Spirit. As Paul warned the Ephesian elders: "Even from your own number men will arise and distort the truth in order to draw away disciples after them" (Acts 20:30).

Likewise, when the Holy Spirit fell on the Toronto Airport Church, a well-known radio personality called it "counterfeit revival." He warned that what was happening in that church fulfilled Jesus' prophecy: "For false Christs and false prophets will appear and perform signs and miracles to deceive the elect" (Mark 13:22). As the Airport Church touched millions of visitors, spread revival worldwide and produced thousands of converts, this opponent warned that the greater its success, the greater its deception.

Remember, Jesus said that as His disciples, we are not above Him. If He was persecuted at the hands of the religious establishment, we too will be persecuted. So how might we experience this type of suffering with Jesus? One way is through social ostracism: "For you have spent enough time in the past doing what pagans choose to do—living in debauchery, lust, drunkenness, orgies, carousing and detestable idolatry. They think it strange that you do not plunge with them into the same flood of dissipation, and they heap abuse on you" (1 Pet. 4:3-4). Jesus promised His followers, "You will be handed over to the local councils and flogged in the synagogues. On account of me you will stand before governors and kings as witnesses to them" (Mark 13:9).

Because we live with Constitutional freedom of religion, I have never been arrested for my faith. But as an evangelical, I have experienced clear opposition from the academic community. In major secular universities on the East Coast, I was always in a small and often misunderstood minority. But when I joined the faculty of Claremont Men's College (now Claremont MacKenna College) in California, I faced my greatest test.

Some of the Claremont faculty had a strong bias that an evangelical could not be an academic person. Historic faith (which they regarded as "fundamentalist") belonged back in the Middle Ages. So they organized to have me fired. Late night meetings were secretly held. I was charged with evangelizing in the classroom. My accusers were nameless. Inferences—based on bias, not on fact— were made against me. This was my first real experience of persecution from this world system, in particular, the secular academic world. I was shocked and amazed. Where was "liberal education"? But then Jesus' warnings hit home:

If the world hates you, keep in mind that it hated me first. If you belonged to the world, it would love you as its own. As it is, you do not belong to the world, but I have chosen you out of the world. That is why the world hates you. Remember the words I spoke to you: "No servant is greater than his master." If they persecuted me, they will persecute you also. . . . In this world you will have trouble. But take heart! I have overcome the world (John 15:18-20; 16:33).

The siege lifted when some faculty (including a Jewish professor of political science and a professor of philosophy at the adjoining Pomona College) came to my defense. After this incident, I stayed for 10 years at Claremont.

Suffering, Level Three: Identifying with the Lost

In addition to suffering attacks from His family and this world system, Jesus suffered as He moved to the sick, the demonized and the lost. Unlike the Buddha, who withdrew from the world into meditation and gave his followers an eightfold path to enlightenment, or Mohammed, who increased suffering in the world as he extended his militant faith by the sword, Christ moved into suffering and was filled with compassion (see Mark 1:41). People saw this and "undressed" before Him. They pointed to their blind eyes. They showed Him their leprous limbs. They pulled out their withered arms. They confessed their adultery, their greed, their injustice. Jesus took their suffering into Himself, absorbed it and stopped it.

Following the example of Jesus, rather than protecting ourselves against suffering, we are called to embrace suffering and bring healing in the power of His Spirit. As the world shrinks, our responsibility grows, both personally and corporately. We must care about the AIDS patients in our community and the millions more in

Africa and Asia. We must seek to bring God's healing power to the
world. We must remember that our God is a missionary God and
that we are to heal the sick with Him. As John Wesley once stated,
the whole world is our parish.[1]

We are also to go after the lost, although this will cost us. In
Luke 15:5, Jesus tells of the shepherd who left his 99 sheep to find
1 stray. When the shepherd found it, he brought it back, rejoicing.
Like the shepherd, to find the lost sheep, we will have to go through
the underbrush, experience anxiety during our search and probably
suffer many a sleepless night. But if we are willing to pay the price,
God will lead us to the lost. And He will do so through the relationships that we have with other people.

I once knew a family that attended the Hollywood First Presbyterian Church. Their son, Gary, went off the rails with drugs, but in
a dramatic moment, he came to Christ. His parents asked me to
meet him, which I gladly did. One of Gary's friends, Mark, was the
most notorious drug addict in Westchester, California, at the time.
He was strung out on barbiturates, taking 14 "reds" a day to main-
tain his habit. He had lumps in his arms where he had injected
heroin and missed the vein.

One Saturday, Gary and I went to see Mark. His mother took us
to his bedroom, where we woke him up and began to talk with him
about Jesus. A friendship grew between us, and Mark soon accepted Christ. We got him out of Westchester, moved him in with us,
and then started the process of detoxing him from the drugs.

We decided to do this at a cabin in the mountains. So I left him
at the cabin with some others and returned to Los Angeles. On the
way, I stopped on a whim to see a friend who worked as a probation
officer. When I told her about Mark, she was alarmed and informed
me that I needed to hospitalize him at once. In a panic, I drove back
to the mountains.

No sooner had I arrived at the cabin than Mark went into a seizure, stopped breathing and turned blue. I jumped to the floor, jammed my finger into his clenched jaw and pulled with all my strength until his teeth cut my bone. I was finally able to pry his jaw open, and he sucked in air. The color returned to his face, and we took him to a hospital immediately. Mark survived and ended up becoming a key player in our street ministry. Later, he graduated from UCLA and went on to receive his Ph.D. from Fuller Theological School of Psychology. (I still have the scar from his teeth!)

Suffering, Level Four: Experiencing the Effects of Sin

In addition to family rejection, persecution and suffering for the lost, we enter into Christ's passion by living in a fallen world. Sin has consequences and we are not immune from them. Paul tells us that as a sign of God's wrath against sin, He lets our sinful actions run their course. What we reap, we will sow (see Rom. 1:18). If we sow to the flesh, we will reap corruption. If we sow to the spirit, we will reap eternal life (see Gal. 6:7-8).

Why do bad things happen to "good" people? Because evil at its core is irrational, we will never have a final answer to that question in this life. However, one truth—which can be cold—is that none of us are "good" in the sense of being perfect or undeserving of God's judgment. We all inherit a fallen nature and the accumulative effects of generational sin.

But what are we to say about babies born with AIDS or babies who are born addicted to drugs because of the actions of their parents? What are we to say of mass victims of a tsunami or hurricanes roaring in off the coast? What are we to say of the tens of thousands of lives taken by famine in Africa or by earthquakes in China? We are not living in Eden, but in a fallen world. We are within God's providential care, but there is an arena of chaos in which Satan is allowed to wreak havoc. Let's also not forget that one reason God allows sin to run its course is to get our attention. C. S. Lewis said that suffering is God's megaphone to rouse a deaf world.[2] How many people have come to Christ out of their "undeserved" suffering?

When I think of the consequences of living in a fallen world, I think of Bob Burgin, the CEO of a Fortune 500 company who had taken an early retirement and moved to California. A southern gentleman, Bob had become a Christian at a Billy Graham Crusade while attending college in Tennessee. He was a generous man, an elder in his church, and served on the Board of Trustees at Fuller Theological Seminary.

However, during his retirement years, Bob became ill. At the end of World War II, he had observed several atomic bomb tests and was apparently infected by radiation fallout. In his final years, inoperable tumors began to appear in his brain. He finally became a quadriplegic and had the use of only one hand. His son, Chris, moved from the East Coast to care for him and run his affairs. Chris had a special handicapped home built for his father's comfort and provided 24-hour nursing care for him.

One Saturday morning, Chris called me. "Dad almost died last night," he said. "Would you go and see him?" I raced to the house and walked into Bob's bedroom. Bob greeted me with a giant smile. I had never seen him so joyful before. He said, "I died last night and went to heaven. I saw Jesus, and He gave me a new name. I was filled with glory. But then I heard my son, Chris, way far away calling, 'Dad, wake up! Dad, wake up!' I knew that I had to come back and tell him. Don, this was the greatest experience of my life."

Believe me, Bob had experienced many great events in his life. He had golfed with several U.S. presidents (one had even asked him to become Secretary of Defense). He had traveled the world in luxury with top business leaders. But that Friday night, by Bob's own report, seeing Jesus and tasting heaven was his greatest experience. He died a few weeks later in complete peace.

I share these stories with you to demonstrate the fact that this is a fallen world. Neither of these men was immune from it, but in the midst of their suffering, Jesus transformed them. As Francis MacNutt reminds us, death is the ultimate healing before we receive our resurrection bodies.[3]

Suffering, Level Five: Battling the Evil One

As we have seen, Jesus taught His disciples to pray, "Deliver us from the evil one" (Matt. 6:13). He lived out what He taught as He delivered people from demons. He then interceded for them in the battle, saying, "My prayer is not that you take them out of the world but that you protect them from the evil one" (John 17:15).

Praying for deliverance is a dark, ugly task. Often we feel the presence of the enemy. The room may grow cold, victims may look vacantly at us or their eyes may roll back, and confusion may rage. We may not always succeed—at least not immediately. In addition, there seems to be a hierarchy of evil. While all of us can deal with lesser spirits in Jesus' name, some spirits need to be addressed by people with strong spiritual authority and experience in deliverance. I have encountered spirits of addiction, anger, lust, homosexuality, witchcraft, religion, rejection and the occult along with other unnamed dark presences. When we pray for deliverance from such spirits, we enter into the combat that took Jesus to the cross. The enemy beat at Christ all the way, and he will, at times, try to do the same to us.

I experienced this when the drummer in our worship band asked me to pray for him for deliverance. Normally, I like to do this in a team, with intercessors nearby. However, in this instance, while I had my intercessors, I was alone for the actual praying. We went for it anyway, and several spirits left. The last one was a religious spirit. I bound any other lurking spirits in Jesus' name, asked the Holy Spirit to come, looked into my friend's open eyes and said, "Religious spirit, I command you to leave now in the name of Jesus and go to Jesus to be dealt with by Him." In a mean, ugly voice, the spirit spoke back to me, "You can't cast me out; you have the same spirit."

I was staggered. I was being beat up. The thought flashed through my mind that the spirit could be right. Then the next thought that occurred to me (the correct one) was that the devil is a liar and the father of lies. I responded, "I don't take counsel from demons. You are a lying spirit and I command you to go now in Jesus' name." With small convulsions, the spirit left, and it was over. My friend was free. I then laid hands on him and asked the Holy Spirit to fill any place left vacant by the spirits' departures. But I continued to wonder, *Do I have a religious spirit?* Finally, I dumped the thought under Jesus' blood and let Him wash it away.

So, sharing in Christ's sufferings includes doing battle against the enemy and his demons. In the end, Jesus Himself experienced not only the flight of His disciples but also the assaults of Satan. This was forever epitomized in Judas. In John 13, Jesus prophesied His betrayer's presence at the Passover meal. John, the beloved disciple, asked, "Lord, who is it?" (v. 25). Jesus answered, "'It is the one whom I will give this piece of bread when I have dipped it in the dish" (v. 26). Jesus then handed it to Judas Iscariot. As soon as Judas took the bread, Satan entered into him (see vv. 26-27).

This is a real battle. John later writes, "Dear friends, do not believe every spirit, but test the spirits to see whether they are from God" (1 John 4:1). Peter warns, "Your enemy the devil prowls around like a roaring lion looking for someone to devour" (1 Pet. 5:8). Paul exhorts us to take up the shield of faith so that we "can extinguish all the flaming arrows of the evil one" (Eph. 6:16). He told the

Thessalonians, "For we wanted to come to you—certainly I, Paul, did, again and again—but Satan stopped [literally "road-blocked"] us" (2:18). Again, he told the church under persecution, "I was afraid that in some way the tempter might have tempted you and our efforts might have been useless" (3:5).

Paul told the Colossians that he completes what is lacking in Christ's sufferings (see 1:24). Objectively, Jesus' suffering for sin was finished on the cross. However, subjectively, He still suffers through His Body as we engage the pain and battle for this world. But Paul promises that we won't suffer alone. As we suffer with Jesus, we will be glorified with Him (see Rom. 8:17).

How then do we put the triumphant Warrior King and the humiliated Suffering Servant together? It all has to do with the Kingdom. As the Warrior King, Jesus drove out demons and healed the sick. However, if that was all He had done, we would have the perfect revelation of the Kingdom but still not be free from our sins, and we would go to hell. So Jesus went as the Suffering Servant to the cross to defeat our final enemies: sin, Satan and death itself (through His resurrection). Indeed, from the cross He is King of the Jews and King of the Cosmos.

In the meantime, we share in Christ's authority and in His suffering. Welcome to the war! Jesus fought it. Paul fought it. Why do we think we get off? Remember, we're in the Kingdom now. We enter through the gate marked "Suffer with Him."

CHAPTER 13

THE SUFFERING KING

As we saw in the last chapter, Jesus suffers *with* us. But He also suffers *for* us. And He does this uniquely and alone. On the cross, He was abandoned, not simply by us, but also by His Father. We will never fully understand the depths of this, but we must try.

CONTEXT: SIN AND SHAME

To step backward for a moment, we all know that we live shame-based lives.[1] This is a result of the Fall. We were created in God's image for relationship and rulership. We were designed to love God, love each other, and care for this planet. In the same way that an earthly king represents his sovereignty by placing an image of himself in his land, so God represented His sovereignty by placing humans, made in His image, on this planet.

We were created to exercise His Kingdom reign over the earth and tend the Garden (see Gen. 2). God also set a boundary for us. In the Garden of Eden, He made all the trees available to Adam and Eve for food except one: the tree of the knowledge of good and evil. God told them that if they ate of that tree, they would die (see Gen. 2:16-17). As long as our original parents lived in intimacy and dependency upon God, they spontaneously and freely lived out "your kingdom come, your will be done on earth as it is in heaven" (Matt. 6:10).

We were created in God's image as male and female. Man's loneliness was banished when God created woman. Our sexuality is fulfilled in a permanent, heterosexual, monogamous union: "For this reason a man will leave his father and mother [permanent] and be united to his wife [heterosexual union], and they will become one flesh [monogamous]" (Gen. 2:24). The final verse of Genesis 2 concludes that our original parents were both naked and unashamed. They were innocent and transparent, in communion with each other and with the God who made them.

But in Genesis 3, everything shatters. The serpent (an instrument of Satan) seduces Adam and Eve. He contradicts God by promising Adam and Eve that if they eat of the tree of the knowledge of good and evil, they will not die. In fact, he says, they will be like God; they will become their own gods (see Gen. 3:5). With this, Adam and Eve rationalize, rebel, eat from the tree, and experience the Fall. Rather than knowing good and evil, they end up simply knowing that they are naked. This triggers their coverup: They make aprons of leaves and jump into the bushes (see vv. 6-8), hiding from each other and from God. In their innocence, Adam and Eve were naked and unashamed. Now, they are naked and ashamed. From this point on, we all live shame-based lives "east of Eden."

What is shame? Gershin Kaufman once wrote:

> [Shame] is the most poignant experience of the self by the self whether felt in humiliation or cowardice or in a sense of failure to cope successfully with challenge. Shame is a wound felt on the inside, dividing us both from ourselves and from one another.[2]

John Bradshaw states:

[Toxic shame] is the source of most of the disturbing inner states that deny full human life. Depression, alienation, self-doubt, isolating loneliness, paranoid and schizoid phenomena, compulsive disorder, splitting of the self, perfectionism, a deep sense of inferiority, inadequacy or failure, the so-called borderline conditions, and disorders of narcissism all result from shame. Shame is a kind of soul murder. Once shame is internalized, it is characterized by a kind of psychic numbness that becomes the foundation for a kind of death in life. Forged in the matrix of our source [family] relationships, shame conditions every other relationship in our lives. Shame is total non-acceptance.[3]

Bradshaw holds that there is an absolute difference between shame and guilt. Guilt says, "I've done something wrong." Shame says, "There is something wrong with me." Guilt says, "What I did is not good." Shame says, "I am no good." It is a being wound, the result of us abandoning God and His abandoning us.[4]

The human race emerges from the Garden shame-based. Our instinctive reaction is to cover up as we go into hiding from each other and from God. We don't want anyone to see us naked, vulnerable or defenseless, so we create a false front. Paul calls this "life in the flesh [our sinful nature]" (Rom. 7:14-25). This is the hole in our souls, the source of all our addictions and compulsions.

However, while we are in hiding, God comes looking for us. He searches us out to break through our shame, forgive us, and fill the emptiness in our soul with Himself. But this never comes at the cost of His righteousness or His justice. We are moral beings, made in His image. His Law governs the universe and is written on our hearts, and through it He establishes the good. As Moses taught the Israelites, keep the Law and be blessed; break it and be cursed (see Deut. 27-28).

Justice demands reward and punishment. Because we are all "law breakers," we deserve punishment. God must uphold His own character as just, even if it means that He must eternally separate Himself from us. But there is more: He is not only absolutely just, but He is also absolutely gracious.

CONTENT: GRACE AND THE GOSPEL

Grace compels God to seek us out and bring us back to Himself. But to be true to Himself, God must satisfy His own justice. He has decreed that the soul that sins must die.

So how can God uphold His justice, punish sin and, at the same time, extend His grace? The answer sends Jesus to the cross. The issue is separation; the answer is restoration. The issue is rejection; the answer is acceptance. The issue is shame; the answer is Jesus who was shamed for us. Through His death He satisfied God's justice and released God's mercy. He paid the price that we will never have to pay, lifting God's wrath from us and welcoming us home free.

Jesus then comes, without shame, and meets us in our shame. He sees every thing we cover up. He sees our divided hearts. He sees our secret lusts. He sees our pornographic fantasies. He sees our selfishness, greed and hypocrisy. He sees what we shove into our unconscious, our psychic wounds, our "amnesia." He sees our denial, our idols, the way we project our problems onto other people. And He is totally welcoming.

Jesus stands on the riverbank with us sinners. He is the man for others and the God for others. He is not afraid to call us "brothers" and "sisters." The wrath that John the Baptist pronounced fell on Him at the cross, and in that awful moment, He shielded us. He is like the hen that gathers her chicks under her wings—even at the cost of her own life.

Here is an example of how Jesus responds to our condition. Imagine you are sitting at the end of a pier when a man comes rushing down, crying, "I love you! I love you!" He jumps into the swirling waters and is carried away. If you saw this, you would think the man was crazy. Now imagine that you fell off the end of the pier and were being carried away by the swirling waters. This same man comes rushing down, crying, "I love you! I love you!" He jumps into the water and pulls you out. If this occurred, you would be forever grateful to this individual.

Jesus took our place by jumping into the swirling waters of judgment and death, and we love Him for it. "Let us fix our eyes on Jesus, the author and perfecter of our faith, who for the joy set before him endured the cross, scorning its shame, and sat down at the right hand of the throne of God" (Heb. 12:2).

The World's Rejection

When Jesus went through His final hours on Earth, He experienced the world's rejection and the Father's acceptance. On His road to the cross, and even in His cry of dereliction ("My God, My God, why have you forsaken me?" [Mark 15:24]), He still remained under the Father's blessing and benediction: "You are my Son, whom I love; with you I am well pleased" (Luke 3:22).

Through the Jewish and Roman trials, Jesus experiences, in microcosm, the rejection of the whole world. The priests and the soldiers try to shame Him. They hound Him. They pick at Him and poke Him. They rage at Him and spit on Him. They beat Him and cut Him. They grab their whips and lash His body until it bleeds. They press thorns into His skull. They laugh, hoot, holler, jeer and belittle Him.

The Roman soldiers use Jesus to vent their pent-up anger. They have to live among strange Jews, stuck in the backwater region of Palestine. They have to handle one Messianic pretender after another. So they throw everything they have at Jesus and take all that He has from Him. They take His dignity, His modesty, His humanity. They strip Him naked and nail Him up for the world to see. They surround Him with bleeding, dying criminals. They hang a mocking sign that reads "King of the Jews" on His cross. As N. T. Wright says, "Crucified Messiahs . . . were failed Messiahs."[5]

This is what the religious leaders and the soldiers do to the Son of God. After condemning Jesus for blasphemy, the Jews shame Him for His *prophetic ministry*. They blindfold Him, strike Him and challenge Him. "If you are a prophet, tell us who hit you. Prophesy now, Jesus" (see Luke 22:63-64). Yet while the full weight of their wrath falls upon Him, He is still held by the Father: "You are my Son, whom I love."

After Jesus' condemnation by Pilate, the Roman governor, the soldiers shame Him for His *kingly ministry*. They clamp on the crown of thorns, drive the spikes in, dress Him in a purple robe and proclaim, "Hail, King of the Jews" (Matt. 27:29). There He is, the rightful ruler of the universe, mocked and shamed. Yet again, He is held by the Father: "You are my Son, whom I love."

Finally, as Jesus hangs on the cross, He is shamed for His *priestly ministry*. The crowd yells, "If you are the Savior, come down from the cross now, Jesus, and we will believe . . . He saved others, but he can't save himself" (Mark 15:31). This was exactly correct: He was savings others by *not* saving Himself, but this the crowd cannot understand. So Jesus dies as the Lamb of God who takes away the sin of the world, but He dies under the barrage of their curses and taunts. Nevertheless, He is held by the Father—"You are my Son, whom I love"—until one final, awful moment.

The Father's Rejection

Jesus, the eternal Son, absolutely secure in the Father's love, now freely and fully steps into the place of shame where we live in ultimate isolation and loneliness. He is the Just One who stands in for us, the unjust. As He does so, the full weight of sin and judgment falls on His righteous body. What happened in Eden is reversed at Calvary. In a moment in time, He takes our eternal shame, our eternal loneliness and our eternal separation on Himself. "My God, my God, why have you forsaken me?" He cries (Mark 15:34).

What does His cry mean? First, we can't possibly know, because even in our shame we are never rejected by God. When Adam and Eve were expelled from Eden, God clothed them to protect them (see Gen. 3:21). He continued the human race through them. In His providence, He makes the sun shine and the rain fall on the just and the unjust. While we are yet sinners, Christ died for us.

But on the cross, Jesus entered into that place of ultimate rejection, loneliness and shame. He hung on the cross of shame, in the place of our shame, for us shameful, shame-driven and shaming creatures. To be sure, some of the shame He felt was due to His hanging naked as a condemned criminal. But deeper still, His shame went into the place of us sinners experiencing the righteous judgment of God and that ultimate separation on our behalf. In the cross there was a wound in the very heart of God. He who knew no sin became sin for us. He is the Lamb of God who takes away the sin of the world.

Second, Jesus' cry was not directed to us. It was "overheard," so we are always at a distance when we reflect on it. In the question, "My God, my God, why have you forsaken me?" we peek into the inner relationship of the Triune God. The Father is in the Son and the Son is in the Father. Jesus was no innocent third party taking the rap for us. The consequences of sin, the separation in that moment, hurt the Father's heart every bit as much as the Son's.

Third, Jesus' cry was from Psalm 22:1, a prophetic psalm that described His crucifixion in detail. But this psalm was also one of vindication. So, the cry points beyond itself to final triumph and resolution. It has been suggested that Jesus prayed this whole psalm from the cross, or that He cried the first verse to point us to the whole text. Listen to some of it:

All who see me mock me;
they hurl insults, shaking their heads:
"He trusts in the Lord;
let the Lord rescue Him . . ." (vv. 6-8)

I am poured out like water,
and all my bones are out of joint.
My heart has turned to wax;
it has melted away within me.
My strength is dried up like a potsherd,
and my tongue sticks to the roof of my mouth;
you lay me in the dust of death (vv. 14-15).

Dogs have surrounded me;
a band of evil men has encircled me,
they have pierced my hands and my feet.
I can count all my bones;
people stare and gloat over me.
They divide my garments among them
and cast lots for my clothing (vv. 16-18).

But you, O Lord, be not far off;
O my Strength, come quickly to help me.
Deliver my life from the sword (vv. 19-20).

I will declare your name to my brothers;
in the congregation I will praise you (v. 22).

For he has not despised or disdained
the suffering of the afflicted one;
He has not hidden his face from him
but has listened to his cry for help (v. 24).

Jesus pays sin's price, cancels our guilt, and breaks through our shame with His love. Regardless of the messages we have heard, the pronouncements of shame on us or the exhortations to shame, Jesus is here. The Father's word to Him is for us in Him: "You are my son, whom I love." "You are my daughter, whom I love." "With you I am well pleased." Welcome home! You can now pray and live out "Your Kingdom come, your will be done, on earth as it is in heaven."

CHAPTER 14

KINGDOM PARADOX: DEATH AND RESURRECTION

In Jesus' Kingdom ministry, God's reign is breaking in on this present sorry planet. All our enemies are being defeated; every area of life is coming under His lordship. The heart of this, as we have seen, is the overthrow of Satan, the great rebel. His demons are sent packing. His lies are exposed.

For the kingdom of God to be within reach and triumph, the Davidic Warrior-King must become the Suffering Servant of the Lord. In this role, Jesus must go to Jerusalem to disarm the devil and die for our sins. However, as N. T. Wright has noted, for most first-century Jews, death was not a one-way street; it was a U-turn.[1] So, Jesus dies. His crucified body is wrapped and buried. He is placed in a borrowed tomb. Then early on Sunday morning, Jesus makes a U-turn. He comes back from the dead, resurrected and re-embodied, and everything is irrevocably changed.

THE NATURE OF RESURRECTION

In Judaism, there was preparation for resurrection to occur but no precedent. Jesus' resurrection prophecies were virtually unintelligible to His disciples and to the Jews. This is because, while most Jews believed in the resurrection of the body, they believed that this resurrection was to be a corporate event at the end of history. What Martha said to Jesus before He raised Lazarus from the grave summed up the popular opinion: "I know he will rise again in the resurrection at the last day" (John 11:24).

The idea that one person would be raised alone before the resurrection at the last day wrenched open the whole category of "resurrection." All the Jews knew was that no single person had ever been raised from the dead, incorruptible and glorified. True, Jesus had brought several people back to life, but this was not the resurrection as the Jews understood it. It was resuscitation, signs of the Kingdom come but nothing more. All those who had been raised from the dead would one day die again. New resurrection bodies would only be given when all the dead were raised in one cataclysmic event at the end of this age. For the Jews, the recreation of all things lay in the future—that is, until that Easter morning when that final, irreversible transformation began.

EVIDENCE FOR JESUS' RESURRECTION

Jesus' resurrection was welded to this general concept of the resurrection of the dead. He was the "first fruits" of the whole deal (see 1 Cor. 15:20). Resurrection was not simply overcoming death; it was part of the bigger picture, the new heavens and the new earth. As Paul says, creation now groans in the agony of childbirth, but one day "the creation itself will be liberated from its bondage to decay and brought into the glorious freedom of the children of God" (Rom. 8:21).

For the Kingdom to fully come, then, our last great enemy, death itself, must be defeated. This happened when Jesus, in His glorified body, walked out of the tomb, leaving the grave wrappings behind. He then appeared to His disciples for 40 days and ascended to heaven, there to reign at God's right hand. But what evidence do we have that His resurrection occurred?

The Records of Jesus' Appearances

First, there are the records of Jesus' appearances. All attempts to explain these appearances as wish fulfillment on the part of His disciples ultimately fail. As we have seen, Jesus' disciples had no way to understand the concept of one person being raised from the dead before the general resurrection that would occur at the end of the age. They flee at Jesus' crucifixion and grieve His absence. When Jesus later appears to them, they are overwhelmed. Their whole perception of reality is shattered and has to be remade.

Yet their doubts and fears are overcome by the sheer weight of Jesus' presence. He talks with them. He eats with them. He teaches them. He touches them. He commissions them to take His Kingdom message and ministry to the nations. He assures them that the Spirit will empower them to do this. He promises His return and then is taken into glory. Fearful, beaten disciples are transformed by meeting the risen Lord, by being forgiven and by being restored and filled with His Spirit. No fake plot or psychological disorder can account for their transformation and the rise of the Early Church.

Again, as N. T. Wright says, "A crucified Messiah is a failed Messiah." The disciples would never have imagined Jesus' resurrection. Like other Messianic movements, they might have appointed another leader to carry the work on or recruited a family member to take Jesus' place. But they would never have proclaimed that Jesus had been raised from the dead, that death was a defeated enemy, and that the general resurrection of the dead had begun with Him. They would never sign that faith with their own bloody deaths—unless they had actually met the risen Lord.

The Empty Tomb

Second, along with Jesus' appearances, there is the supporting evidence of the empty tomb. If Jesus' enemies could have produced His body they would have, and His movement would have been immediately over. However, they didn't, because they couldn't. In addition, Jesus' disciples would have never stolen His body and faked His resurrection. Apart from the moral issues involved, as we have mentioned, they simply had no category into which to fit a single resurrection. They might have said that Jesus lived on in their hearts or that He had gone to heaven, but to say that He had been raised from the dead didn't fit their theology or their understanding of reality (their worldview).

The uniqueness of Christianity lies in Jesus' incarnation, His bringing the Kingdom, His death for sin, and His resurrection from the dead. Christianity is resurrection faith, grounded in history, or it is nothing. It breaks apart all our psychological, sociological, theological, historical and spiritual categories. Listen to Paul's polemic:

> But if it is preached that Christ has been raised from the dead, how can some of you say that there is no resurrection of the dead? [Because you are dualists and believe that salvation is liberation from this evil, materialistic world rather than its transformation.] If there is no resurrection of the dead, then not even Christ has been raised. And if Christ has not been raised, our preaching is useless [in vain] and so is your faith. More than that, we are then found to be false witnesses about God [liars], for we have testified about God [given law-court witness] that he raised Christ from the dead. But he did not raise him if in fact the

dead are not raised [as the Greeks hold]. For if the dead are not raised, then Christ has not been raised either [your Hellenistic worldview excludes it by your anti-body assumptions]. And if Christ has not been raised, your faith is futile [vain, empty]; you are still in your sins. Then those also who have fallen asleep [died] in Christ are lost. If only for this life we have hope in Christ, we are to be pitied more than all men. But Christ has indeed been raised from the dead, the firstfruits [the beginning of the general resurrection of the dead] of those who have fallen asleep [died] (1 Cor. 15:12-20).

The Transformation of the Cross

Third, we must add the transformation of the cross to the evidence of Jesus' resurrection. When Jesus died, everyone believed that it was over. He endured the most sadistic means of Roman justice. The cross was an offense to the ancient world. It was described as the "barren wood," "the slave's punishment."[2] Under Roman law, no Roman citizen could be crucified. It was the most severe form of capital punishment because it included humiliation, torture and death. Every major city had its place of crucifixion. After the slave revolt in Rome, the major highway into the city was lined with thousands of crucified rebels. When Titus seized Jerusalem, he crucified Jews daily around the walls until he ran out of wood. This controlled terror was designed to aid in crime prevention as well as crime punishment.

Crucifixion was not to be mentioned in polite company. Cicero writes, "Let even the name of the cross be kept away not only from the bodies of the citizens of Rome, but also from their thought, sight and hearing."[3] According to one legend, when a man went to the god Apollo to find out how to dissuade his wife from

Christianity, the god replied, "Let her continue as she pleases, persisting in her vain delusions, and lamenting in song a god who died in delusions, who was condemned by judges whose verdict was just, and executed in the prime of life by the worst of deaths, a death bound with iron."

After surveying ancient evidence, Martin Hengel finds varying forms of "abhorrence at the new religious teaching. . . . The heart of the Christian message, which Paul described as the 'word of the cross,' ran counter not only to Roman political thinking, but to the whole ethos of religion in ancient times and in particular to the ideas of God held by educated people."[4]

In contrast to the Greek myths, "to believe that the one pre-existent Son of the one true God, the mediator at creation and the redeemer of the world, had appeared in very recent times in out-of-the-way Galilee as a member of the obscure people of the Jews, and even worse, had died the death of a common criminal on the cross, could only be regarded as a sign of madness."[5] Further, "a crucified Messiah, son of God or God must have seemed a contradiction in terms to anyone, Jew, Greek, Roman or barbarian, asked to believe such a claim, and it will certainly have been thought offensive and foolish."[6]

Seneca asks, "Can anyone be found who would prefer wasting away in pain dying limb by limb, or letting out his life drop by drop, rather than expiring once for all? Can any man be found willing to be fastened to the accursed tree, long sickly, already deformed, swelling with ugly weals on shoulders and chest, and drawing the breath of life amid long-drawn-out agony?"[7] Seneca implies that the answer is no. But the Christians answered, "Yes." There was one who could be found who would go through all of this and more, one who would bear the full weight of human sin and shame in His bloody death.

THE POWER OF THE CROSS

But how can we know that Jesus' death was the once-for-all sacrifice for sin? How can we know that the judge of all the earth had become the victim of His own justice to free the unjust and give them eternal life? How can we know that the Father accepted the sacrifice of His Son on our behalf? How do we know that the price is paid in full on our account?

We know because Jesus has been raised from the dead. He is alive. His cross is vindicated—not as the place of humiliation and loss, but as the place of sacrifice and atonement. Paul puts it this way: "He [Christ] was delivered over to death of our sins and was raised to life for our justification" (Rom. 4:25).

The resurrection then validates the cross. It also means that the cross, however repulsive and distasteful to Jew and Greek, is the heart of the full Kingdom message. There, the price of sin is paid. There, our final enemies are defeated. There, the crucified Son of God reigns.

For us, Christ crucified is the power of God. Through the cross, sin is cancelled, Satan is defeated and, in the resurrection, death is conquered. When we come to the Cross, bow there, confess our sins and receive the crucified Lord, we receive the assurance that our sins are forgiven, our conscience is cleared, our hearts are cleansed and that God has stamped "not guilty" on our account through the blood of His Son.

When we come to the Cross, the judgment of death that should fall on us falls on Jesus, our Passover Lamb (see 1 Cor. 5:7). His resurrection begins our final exodus. Under the banner of the Cross and in the power of His resurrection, we leave Satan's kingdom and enter into the kingdom of God that is come and coming. As Paul says, "For he [God] has rescued us from the dominion of darkness and brought us into the kingdom of the Son he loves, in who we have redemption [Exodus, deliverance], the forgiveness of sins" (Col. 1:13-14).

To meet the risen Lord—to know that His kingdom rules over sin and death—is to live again. But there is one thing more: Jesus now enters into our hearts by His Spirit. This is not simply as presence, but also as power. What happened to Jesus during baptism must happen to us. We all need to have our own personal Pentecost.

CHAPTER 15

KINGDOM POWER

The prophet Ezekiel had a vision in which he saw a valley of dry bones (see Ezek. 37:1-11). The Spirit of God came, put the bones back together, clothed the bones with flesh, and breathed life into them. They stood up and lived again. God told Ezekiel that the dry bones represented the whole house of Israel made new by His Spirit.

In the Old Testament, God promised that He would give His people a new Covenant, a new heart, a new David, a new Temple, a new Jerusalem and a new Law. He would empower them with His Spirit, make them a light to the nations, and raise them from the dead. This is revival.

At its heart, Christianity is a revivalist movement. Literally, the word "revival" means "to wake the dead." Biblical faith, in its deepest analysis, views us as separated from God in trespasses and sins, captive to Satan, and subject to divine wrath (see Eph. 2:1-3). We need to be reborn spiritually and restored to a whole new life. So once we are delivered from Satan's kingdom, we are delivered into God's kingdom. We die with Jesus to our old life and rise to our new life. This is revival.

John the Baptist prepared the people for this by calling them to repent. He excommunicated the whole nation and then called them to a new exodus through baptism in the Jordan River. People were not only cleansed, but they were also delivered to become God's people once again, prepared for their Messiah.

While John baptized with water, he promised that One would come who would baptize with the Holy Spirit. Jesus fulfilled John's movement and replaced it. He too called people to repent. But more than this, He announced the presence of the Kingdom and summoned people into it.

As we come into the Kingdom, we submit to the King. Our salvation is based on the confession, "Jesus is King (Messiah)" or "Jesus is Lord." As we make this confession and believe that God has raised Jesus from the dead, we are saved, or "revived" (see Rom. 10:9). As Jesus lives, so we also live.

The gospel core is that Jesus died and was raised from the dead. In the tomb, He didn't simply need renewal, as if He were sleeping, undernourished or, as some have claimed, drugged. He was dead! He needed resurrection. This is what makes Easter such a joyous celebration. The tomb was empty. Jesus is alive again. And because He lives, so we will also be raised to be like Him on this planet in the new creation begun in His resurrection.

THE COMING OF THE HOLY SPIRIT

Jesus knew both the Spirit's presence and His power. In His baptism, He received power and a regal anointing, and promises that His followers will receive the same. What happened to Jesus would happen to them and, likewise, will happen to us.

After the resurrection, the risen Lord commanded His followers to wait in Jerusalem. He told them, "I am going to send you what my Father has promised; but stay in the city until you have been clothed with power from on high" (Luke 24:49). Two things must be said here. First, Jesus' disciples were to experience the Triune God. Their destiny was to be incorporated into the very life of the Trinity. By grace alone, they were to become "partakers of the divine nature" and connected to the living God (see 2 Pet. 1:4). Second, they were to receive Jesus' power to do His works. They anticipated this when Jesus sent them out to preach the Kingdom, cast out demons, heal the sick and liberate the oppressed, but this will now be their full destiny when His Spirit falls on them. As subjects of the King, they will minister the Kingdom.

Like the disciples of a rabbi, Jesus' disciples were extensions of Himself, although more profoundly so. As people dealt with the disciples, so they dealt with Him. As people experienced them, so they experienced Jesus and the Father who sent Him. Through them in Jesus' name (authority), those who believed were set free from Satan's kingdom and entered the kingdom of God. Through the disciples, they experienced healing and deliverance that began the restoration of all things. Through them, God's kingdom would come and His will would be done on Earth as it is in heaven.

Like Jesus, the disciples would also minister in the tension of the Kingdom come and coming. They knew both Jesus' power and Jesus' sufferings as they rescued people from this present evil age (see Gal. 1:4). They were the instruments of the final exodus, ushering all the nations into the Promised Land of the new heavens and the new earth.

WAIT FOR THE POWER

The disciples now knew the risen Lord and had received His forgiveness. They saw the cross not as a failure but as a victory. They were basking in worship and prayer. But they needed something more—the power of the Spirit.

Once again, the risen Lord commanded them, "Do not leave Jerusalem, but wait for the gift my Father promised, which you have heard me speak about. For John baptized with water, but in a few days you will be baptized [flooded, immersed] with the Holy Spirit" (Acts 4:1). Later, when the disciples asked Jesus about restoring the Kingdom to Israel, He answered, "It is not for you to know the times or dates the Father has set by his own authority. But you will receive power when the Holy Spirit comes on you; and you will be my witnesses in Jerusalem, and in all Judea and Samaria, and to the ends of the earth" (Acts 1:7-8).

Jesus then ascended into heaven. As the disciples looked up into the sky where He had gone, two angels suddenly appeared and promised that He would return. Meanwhile, the apostles, Jesus' mother, Mary, the other women and Jesus' brothers met in an upper room to pray (see Acts 1:14). In the interim, they replaced Judas, restoring the magic number of the apostles to 12, and then waited in expectant obedience.

A 10-day gap separated Jesus' ascension into heaven from the coming of the Spirit in power at Pentecost (a major Jewish harvest feast). We can imagine them praying and counting the days as they wonder when they will receive the power that Jesus promised. Did they become discouraged? Did they start to doubt Jesus? Or were they too busy worshiping the Lord and repenting over past failures? We don't know, but Luke does tell us that they prayed constantly.

Then, on the tenth day, the Spirit fell upon them. The risen Lord's promise that they would be immersed with the Spirit and that the Spirit would come upon them would now be their experience rather than simply their hope. This is the secret of Pentecost. And remember, the power was given to them for a mission: They were to be witnesses to Jesus from Jerusalem, to Samaria and to the ends of the earth.

The Spirit's empowering completed what James Dunn calls the "salvation package."[1] Peter promised this at the end of his Pentecost sermon: "Repent and be baptized, every one of you, in the name [authority] of Jesus Christ for the forgiveness of your sins. And you will receive the gift of the Holy Spirit" (Acts 2:38). This would be their final exodus from Satan's kingdom and God's wrath.

As we have already said, it is presumptuous to think that we can do what Jesus did without His power. Apart from this power, our faith becomes simply moralistic (a list of rules) or stoic (we just hang in there until Jesus returns). We need the whole life of the Triune God working in us. Sadly, as A. W. Tozer states, most Christians are Trinitarian only as a formality. If the Spirit left their churches, everything would go on as usual![2]

The "normal" Christian life, then, is lived in the power of the Spirit. In Galatians 3:5, Paul asked, "Does God give you his Spirit and work miracles among you because you observe the law, or because you believe what you heard?" If we were to ask many Christians this same question today, they would probably give us a blank stare. "What Spirit? What miracles?" they might well reply. But, just like Jesus Himself, Paul always evangelized in the Spirit's power. He reminded the Corinthians, "My message and my preaching were not with wise and persuasive words, but with a demonstration of the Spirit's power, so that your faith might not rest on men's wisdom but on God's power" (2:4-5).

RECEIVE THE POWER

The coming of the Spirit at Pentecost was not the coming of the Spirit *and* power but the coming of the Spirit *as* power.[3] The Spirit came with a rush of wind, tongues of fire and an explosion of praise: "All of them [in the Upper Room] were filled with the Holy Spirit and began to speak in other tongues as the Spirit enabled them" (Acts 2:4).

As the apostles broke out into the streets with their new gift of languages, the mixed multitude heard them praising God in their own tongues. In the commotion, some of the bystanders accused them of being drunk (see v. 13). Peter responded by saying that what they are seeing and hearing was the fulfillment of the prophet Joel's promise that the Spirit would be poured on them:

> In the last days, God says, "I will pour out my Spirit on all people. Your sons and daughters will prophesy, your young men will see visions, and your old men will dream dreams. Even on my servants, both men and women, I will pour out my Spirit in those days, and they will prophesy. I will show wonders in the heaven above and signs on the earth below. . . . And everyone who calls on the name of the Lord will be saved" (Acts 2:17-21).

In the power of the Spirit, Peter then preached Jesus: His life, His death, His resurrection and His reign. On that day, 3,000 were converted and baptized (see Acts 2:41). They too received "the gift of the Holy Spirit" (2:38).

The Jewish Pentecost was followed by the Samaritan Pentecost. Philip the Evangelist traveled to Samaria to proclaim Christ to the people there, and many embraced the faith. Soon after, Peter and John came down from Jerusalem to lay hands on them, and they also received the Holy Spirit (see Acts 8:17). The Samaritan Pentecost was followed by the Gentile Pentecost, in which Peter preached to the Roman officer Cornelius and his household. The Spirit fell on the household in the middle of his sermon:

> While Peter was still speaking these words [of the gospel], the Holy Spirit came upon all who heard the message.

The circumcised [Jewish] believers who had come with
Peter were astonished that the gift of the Holy Spirit had
been poured out even on the Gentiles. For they heard them
speaking in tongues and praising God (Acts 10:44-46).

In shock, Peter concluded that they must be baptized in water
because they "have received the Holy Spirit just as we have" (v. 47).
Later, he reported to Jerusalem that the Spirit had fallen on the
Gentiles just as He had fallen on the Jewish believers (see 11:1-17).

The argument has been advanced that these are all unique and
unrepeatable events, fulfilling the promise in Acts 1:8 that the gospel
will go from Jerusalem to Samaria and then to the ends of the earth
(as symbolized by the Gentile Cornelius). Proponents of this view-
point argue that the purpose of these signs and wonders was to
prove that Jesus was the Son of God and to authenticate the apostle's authority and that the canon of Scripture, the preaching of
God's Word and the celebration of the sacraments now take their
place. In other words, we shouldn't expect Pentecostal power and
signs and wonders—that was for them then, but not for us today. Yet
the book of Acts and witness of Church history fail to support this
narrow position.

WITNESSES TO THE POWER

The Jerusalem Church, under persecution, prayed for God to give
its members boldness in evangelism and to release signs and wonders (miracles) in their ministry. After this, Luke reports that the
house in which the disciples were staying was shaken and they were
all filled with the Holy Spirit (see 4:31). To Luke, the filling of the
Spirit was not simply for the birthday of the Church or for the
three stages of mission advance. It was for every move of God as He
extended His kingdom.

Likewise, when Paul later found followers of John the Baptist in Ephesus, he asked them, "Did you receive the Holy Spirit when you believed?" (Acts 19:2). When they replied, "No, we have not even heard that there is a Holy Spirit," Paul shared the gospel with them, and they were baptized in the name of Jesus. Luke then reports, "When Paul placed his hands on them, the Holy Spirit came on them, and they spoke in tongues and prophesied" (v. 6). For Luke, this was clearly a normative and repeatable Christian experience.

Early-Church Fathers

Kingdom ministry later drove the Church into the Roman world. Whenever revival came or mission advanced, signs and wonders were performed in the name of Jesus. Listen to the witness of Irenaeus, a Church Father in the latter quarter of the second century, on deliverance:

> Others have foreknowledge of things to come; they see visions, and utter prophetic expressions. Others still, heal the sick by laying their hands upon them, and they are made whole. Yea, moreover, as I have said, the dead even have been raised up, and remained among us for many years. And what more shall I say? It is not possible to name the number of the gifts which the Church, [scattered] throughout the whole world, has received from God, in the name of Jesus Christ. . . . [But] directing her prayers to the Lord, who made all things . . . and calling upon the name of our Lord Jesus Christ, she has been accustomed to work miracles for the advantage of mankind.[4]

In A.D. 731, the Venerable Bede wrote the *Ecclesiastical History of the English People,* in which he recounts the martyrdom of a man named

Alban during the Diocletian persecution in A.D. 303-304. Bede states that Alban "renounced the darkness of idolatry, and sincerely accepted Christ." When ordered by the Roman authorities to sacrifice to the pagan gods, Alban refused, stating that to do so would be to sacrifice to devils "who cannot help their suppliants, nor answer their prayers and vows. On the contrary, whosoever offers sacrifice to idols is doomed to the pains of hell."[5] After Alban was tortured and decapitated, a church was built at the place of his martyrdom. Bede reports that at this church "sick folk are healed and frequent miracles take place to this day."[6]

Bede also recounts the story of Bishop Germanus, whose broken leg was healed by an angel: "And while he refused any treatment for his own illness, he saw beside him one night a being in shining robes, who seemed to reach out his hand and raise him up, ordering him to stand on his feet. From that moment his pain ceased, his former health was restored."[7] After this event, Germanus was confronted by a local chieftain named Elaphius whose son was crippled by a painful disease of the leg so that his muscles were atrophied. Bede reports:

Suddenly Elaphius threw himself at the bishops' feet and, presented to them his son, the sight of whose infirmity proclaimed his need louder than words. All were moved to pity at the spectacle, especially the bishops, who earnestly prayed God to show mercy. Blessed Germanus then asked the youth to sit down, and drawing out the leg bent with disease, he passed his healing hand over the afflicted area, and at his touch health swiftly returned. The withered limb filled, the muscles regained their power, and in the presence of them all the lad was restored healed to his parents. The people were amazed at this miracle, and the Catholic [Universal] Faith was firmly implanted in all their hearts.[8]

Later, Pope Gregory (the Great) sent Augustine of Canterbury to evangelize England. When Gregory heard of the miracles performed through Augustine, he warned him against pride. Here is a part of his letter:

My very dear brother, I hear that Almighty God has worked great wonders through you for the nation which He has chosen. Therefore let your feeling be one of fearful joy and joyful fear at God's heavenly gifts—joy that the souls of the English are being drawn through outward miracles to inward grace; fear lest the frail mind becomes proud because of these wonderful events. Finally, dearest brother, in all the outward actions which by God's help you perform, always strictly examine your inner dispositions. Clearly understand your own character, and how much grace is in this nation for whose conversion God has given you the power to work miracles.[9]

John Wesley and the Evangelical Awakening

Now let's fast forward to John Wesley and eighteenth-century England. Wesley, who was Oxford educated and ordained into the Anglican ministry, preached the gospel throughout the British Isles and led the Evangelical Awakening, a movement that changed the face of the English-speaking world. As he did so, many signs and wonders accompanied his ministry. This, of course, provoked controversy. Were these manifestations simply natural effects, the consequence of a warm room, or what? Wesley reports:

Today, Monday 21 [1739], our Lord answered for himself. For while I was enforcing these words, "'Be still, and know that I am God," He began to make bare his arm, not in a close room, neither in private, but in the open air, and before more than two thousand witnesses. One, and another, and another was struck to the earth; exceedingly trembling at the presence of His power. Others cried with a loud and bitter cry, "What must we do to be saved?" And in less than an hour seven persons, wholly unknown to me till that time, were rejoicing, and singing, and with all their might giving thanks to the God of their salvation.[10]

Controversy over this issue continued to erupt between Wesley and George Whitefield, his companion in field preaching and the leader of the Great Awakening in the American colonies. Wesley recounts:

I had an opportunity to talk with him [Whitefield] of those outward signs which had so often accompanied the inward work of God. I found his objections were chiefly grounded on gross misrepresentations of matter of fact. But the next day he had an opportunity of informing himself better: For no sooner had he begun (in the application of his sermon) to invite all sinners to believe in Christ, than four persons sunk down close to him, almost in the same moment. One of them lay without either sense or motion. A second trembled exceedingly. The third had strong convulsions all over his body, but made no noise, unless by groans. The fourth, equally convulsed, called upon God, with strong cries and tears. From this time, I trust, we shall all suffer God to carry on his own work in the way that pleaseth him.[11]

Wesley and his companions, like the Early Church in Acts, experienced the power of the Spirit again and again. This first happened early New Year's Day in 1739. Wesley reports:

Mr. Hall, Hinching, Ingham, Whitefield, Hutching and my brother Charles were present at our love feast in Fetter Lane with about 60 of our brethren. About 3 in the morning as we were continuing instant in prayer the power of God came mightily upon us, insomuch that many cried out for exulting joy and many fell to the ground. As soon as we were recovered a little from the awe and amazement at the presence of His majesty, we broke out with one voice, "We praise Thee, O God, we acknowledge Thee to be the Lord."

But Pentecost is repeatable. Wesley writes:

We met at Fetter-Lane [where the Spirit first fell on them], to humble ourselves before God, and own he had justly withdrawn his Spirit from us, for our manifold unfaithfulness. We acknowledged our having grieved him by our divisions; "one saying, I am of Paul; another, I am of Apollos": By our leaning again to our own works, and trusting in them, instead of Christ; by our resting in those little beginnings of sanctification, which it had pleased Him to work in our souls; and, above all, by blaspheming his work among us, imputing it either to nature, to the force of imagination and animal spirits, or even to the delusion of the devil. In that hour, we found God with us as at the first. Some fell prostrate upon the ground. Others burst out, as with one consent, into loud praise and thanksgiving. And many openly testified, there had been no such day as this since January the first preceding.[12]

The power of the Spirit led not only to mass evangelism but also to manifestations of Kingdom power through deliverance. For example, Wesley reported having delivered many from demons:

Soon after, I was sent for to one of those who was so strange-
ly torn by the devil, that I almost wondered her relations
did not say, 'Much religion hath made thee mad.' We
prayed God to bruise Satan under her feet. Immediately we
had the petition we asked of Him. She cried out vehement-
ly, 'He is gone, he is gone!' and was filled with the spirit of
love and of a sound mind. I have seen her many times since,
strong in the Lord.[13]

Along with preaching and deliverance, they also healed the sick.
Wesley writes:

I visited many of the sick, and among the rest, J___ W___,
who was in grievous pain both of body and mind. After a
short time spent in prayer, we left her. But her pain was
gone: Her soul being in full peace, and her body also
strengthened, that she immediately rose, and the next day
went abroad. . . . I explained, in the evening, the thirty-
third chapter of Ezekiel: In applying which, I was suddenly
seized with such a pain in my side, that I could not speak. I
knew my remedy, and immediately kneeled down. In a
moment the pain was gone: And the voice of the Lord cried
aloud to sinners, "Why will ye die, O house of Israel?"[14]

Wesley himself reported his healing from an illness that caused
him great pain in his back and head and was accompanied by a
high fever:

I was seized with such a cough, that I could hardly speak.
At the same time came strongly into my mind, "These
signs shall follow them that believe." I called on Jesus

aloud, to "increase my faith"; and to "confirm the word of his grace." While I was speaking, my pain vanished away; the fever left me; my bodily strength returned; and for many weeks I felt neither weakness nor pain. "Unto thee, O Lord, do I give thanks."[15]

Remember, these reports are not from the margins of Christianity. One involves Iraenaus, the best known Church Father before St. Augustine. Another is from Pope Gregory the Great, leader of the Western Church after the fall of Rome. Then another comes from John Wesley, the father of Methodism. In each case, signs and wonders were within their current expectation. While it is true that Kingdom ministry has at times suffered at the hands of worldview shifts, clergy ignorance and immorality, ecclesiastical control, assimilation to magic and the decline of spiritual life, wherever the Church advanced against paganism or went into revival, signs and wonders reappeared. The Church continues to do so today.

The Holy Spirit at Work Today

Let's now fast-forward to our own era. Carol Wimber shared a dream she had in September 1976:

In the dream I was preaching. . . . There was a large crowd. My topic was the gifts of the Holy Spirit. I considered myself an expert on the subject. After all, for years I was responsible for running off members who practice gifts like tongues, healing or prophecy—gifts I considered dangerous and divisive. I was preaching through my well-rehearsed seven-point sermon when, at the final point, a sensation like hot electricity hit my head, traveled down my body, then up and out of my mouth. I awakened speaking in tongues. I was so troubled by the dream and the experience of speaking in tongues that, like a bag of sand with a hole in it, my confidence and self-assurance drained away. "Perhaps," I thought, "I don't know as much as I thought I did about the Christian life . . ." "O God," I cried out, "if all that stuff [meaning spiritual gifts such as tongues and healing] is from you, then I have barely known you all these years." There was a long silence. Then I sensed in my heart a gentle answer: "You're right" . . . Today I look back on that experience as a "personality meltdown," a breaking of my self-will that was so profound I have never been the same since.[16]

Michael Cassidy, founder of African Enterprise, a continent-wide evangelistic movement, was a graduate of Cambridge University and Fuller Theological Seminary who experienced a "second touch" from the Lord after praying in the evening with Michael Nuttall, the then Bishop of Pretoria. He recounts the incident:

Sleep would not come to me. Instead, quite out of the blue, the Spirit of praise came upon my soul. All seemed to be release. All seemed to be freedom. Hour after hour I praised my God in unrestrained and unrestrainable doxology and song. In words of men and angels I rejoiced. No fatigue visited me that night. All my senses were vibrantly alive to God. The Holy Spirit was blessing me. Wave upon wave, it seemed. Flow upon flow. He seemed to be bubbling up from within, surrounding from without, ascending from below and descending from above. Somewhere in the early hours of the morning I said to myself: "I don't know the correct biblical name for this, but this is the experience I've heard others talk of."[17]

And Professor G. Robert Jacks, lately of Princeton Theological Seminary, writes in a personal letter dated February 10, 1997:

I had been corresponding for nearly two years with a young (30 year old) Finnish theology student . . . Marko Jauhiainen by name . . . We've developed a very close brother/father-son relationship. He is a Vineyard person, and in the process of knowing him, many of my Presbyterian blinders were blown away to an awareness of a God considerably more "God" than I had ever experienced.

At one point we began talking about gifts of the Spirit. Not your usual parlor conversation for your typical Presbyterian, I know . . . Last April (the 18th, about 8:30 A.M.) we were chatting on IRC (internet relay chat) . . . about spiritual gifts. He said he had spoken in tongues, and I said I'd never experienced that. Moments later he was saying, essentially, "Shut up, I'm going to pray for you." (He was not that crass.)

What followed was my shaking, weeping, sobbing "Jesus! Jesus! Jesus!", gasping for breath and practically falling out of my chair. I felt this incredible sense of the presence of Christ. An incredible sense of love. And all the while being prayed for over the Internet! Afterward, he said some people would call my experience "baptism in the Spirit," some would call it "being filled with the Spirit," some would call it "being touched by the Spirit." I only knew everything was different from what it had been. Everything.

One of the most remarkable chapters of Church history is now being written in China. After the Communists had expelled the missionaries, closed churches and executed pastors, Mao Tze Tung's wife promised that Christianity would be only a memory in China. She couldn't have been more wrong. Today, it is estimated that the underground Church in China has more than 100 million converts. But how is it that the Church has exploded with no Western resources?

Part of the answer lies in the foundation laid by centuries of mission work. As Jesus promised in His Parable of the Sower, although opposition may take out much seed, the harvest will still come. But the other part of the answer lies in Kingdom ministry, rolling back the darkness and manifesting the power of God.

One account of the Kingdom in China comes from Brother Yun in his book *The Heavenly Man*, published in 2002. As a boy of 16, Yun's father was dying of lung and stomach cancer. A local Daoist priest believed that the father's sickness was the result of upsetting demons, but the priest was unable to cast them out. As a child, Yun's mother had attended a Christian school and learned about God, but most of that knowledge had faded away. Yun recounts:

One night my mother was lying on her bed, barely awake. Suddenly, she heard a very clear and tender, compassionate voice say, "Jesus loves you." She knelt down on the floor and tearfully repented of her sins and re-dedicated herself to the Lord Jesus Christ . . . She immediately called our family to come and pray to Jesus. She told us, "Jesus is the only hope for Father." All of us committed our lives to God when we heard what had happened. We then laid our hands on my father and for the rest of the night we cried out a simple prayer, "Jesus, heal Father! Jesus, heal Father!" The very next morning my father found he was much better! For the first time in months he had an appetite for food. Within a week he had recovered completely and had no trace of cancer! It was a great miracle from God.[18]

Yun's family invited friends and relatives to hear how this had happened. They covered the windows and locked the door of the house before explaining how their father was healed. Yun recounts, "All our relatives and friends knelt down on the floor and gladly accepted Jesus as Lord and Master."[19] Yun's illiterate mother became the village's first preacher and house church pastor. Yun reports, "Some of today's great house church leaders in China first met the Lord through my mother's ministry."[20]

After fasting and praying for 100 days for a Bible, Yun received a vision of two men delivering it to him in a red bag. Almost immediately, these very same men appeared at his door and handed him a Bible—yes, in a red bag. Later, Yun discovered that three months before, an evangelist had received a vision to give his precious, forbidden Bible to Yun.[21] It was like Cornelius and Peter's vision-driven encounter in the book of Acts, reprogrammed for the Chinese Church. After memorizing whole books of his Bible, Yun began to wonder about the Holy Spirit. But his mother was unable to answer his questions. He recalls:

She simply said, "Why don't you pray and ask God for the Holy Spirit just like you prayed for your Bible?" This was a defining moment of my life. I had a desire for God's presence and power, and now I realized how important it is to know God's written Word.

I prayed to the Lord, "I need the power of the Holy Spirit. I am willing to be your witness." After the prayer God's spirit of joy fell upon me. A deep revelation of God's love and presence flooded my being. I'd never enjoyed singing before but many new songs of worship flowed from my lips. They were words I had never learned before. Later, I wrote them down. These songs are still sung in the Chinese house churches to this day.[22]

Yun became a key evangelist and church planter. His life continues to be Spirit-led and prophetically driven. For example, he recounted that 1980 was "a phenomenal year for the church in Henan [Province]. We remember it as the year when God constantly did outstanding miracles and divine healing, and the words of Jesus came supernaturally to many people."[23] This kind of church growth cannot be stopped!

The church of Pentecost and our churches, then, are to be Spirit driven. As we mentioned, that power is given for mission. The promise has been made to us that the Spirit will come to all of God's people. They will prophesy and receive visions and dreams as vehicles of revelation. They will also minister in signs and wonders. The Kingdom come breaks Satan's grip and ushers in the restoration of the fallen creation. The book of Acts and the witness of history document that this day is here.

So when we enter the Kingdom, we pass through the gate marked "Kingdom Power." But how does this work itself out in ministry? We turn now to this.

CHAPTER 16

MANIFESTATIONS OF THE SPIRIT

As with Jesus in His earthly ministry, the Kingdom now advances in His heavenly ministry. In Acts, God extends His reign by the power of His Spirit from Jerusalem to Rome and then to the ends of the earth. Let's look at the Spirit's manifestations as the Church moves.

THE SPIRIT HIMSELF

First, the Spirit, given by the Father and the Son, manifests Himself (see Acts 2:33). The Holy Spirit empowers and executes God's mission. Although the book of Acts is really the book of the risen Lord continuing His ministry through the Spirit, nevertheless, there are many references to the Spirit's unmediated power and direction. For example: "Then Peter, filled with the Holy Spirit, said . . ." (4:8); "And they were all filled with the Holy Spirit and spoke the word of God boldly" (4:31); "But Stephen, full of the Holy Spirit, looked up to heaven and saw the glory of God" (7:55); "The Spirit told Philip, 'Go to that chariot and stay near it'" (8:29); "While they were worshiping the Lord and fasting, the Holy Spirit said, 'Set apart for me

Barnabas and Saul'" (13:2); So the narrative goes, Spirit-filled and Spirit-led.

Today, people often make the similar claim that the Spirit speaks to them and leads them. Whether this is just a formula, a fantasy or a real experience is, at times, hard to discern. Language is often imprecise as well: Someone may say, "The Lord spoke to me," when accuracy demands, "The Spirit spoke to me" or "The Lord spoke to me through His Spirit." The conclusion rests on whether the speaker is a credible witness, whether his or her experience is in accord with Scripture, and whether he or she is in submission to a body of believers.

ANGELS

In addition to the Spirit's direct work, angels are often sent from God's throne as His messengers and agents. Angels appear early in Acts when they announce to the disciples that the risen and ascended Lord will return as He departed—in glory: "[The disciples] were looking intently up into the sky as he [Jesus] was going, when suddenly two men dressed in white stood beside them. 'Men of Galilee,' they said, 'why do you stand here looking into the sky? This same Jesus, who has been taken from you into heaven, will come back in the same way you have seen him go into heaven'" (Acts 1:10-11). It is possible that these are the same angels that met the women at the empty tomb (see Luke 24:4-7).

In Acts 5:20, when the apostles are arrested, an angel opens the prison doors during the night. The angel commands the apostles, "Go, stand in the temple courts . . . and tell the people the full message of this new life." Again, in Acts 8:26, an angel directs Philip to evangelize an Ethiopian eunuch: "Now an angel of the Lord said to Philip, 'Go south to the road—the desert road—that goes down from Jerusalem to Gaza.'" Later, in Acts 10:3, an angel appears to the Roman centurion Cornelius in a vision: "He distinctly saw an angel of God, who came to him and said, 'Cornelius!'"

In Acts 12:7, Peter is arrested, bound and thrown into prison. "Suddenly an angel of the Lord appeared and a light shone in the cell." Awakening Peter, the angel releases him from his chains and commands Peter to dress and follow him out of the prison. Luke reports that Peter thinks it is all a vision. Once on the street, the angel suddenly departs and Peter is left alone: "Then Peter came to himself and said, 'Now I know without a doubt that the Lord sent his angel and rescued me from Herod's clutches and from everything the Jewish people were anticipating'" (12:11).

From these accounts it is apparent that angels were frequent visitors to the faithful in the Early Church. But are the heavens still open today? Otto Piper, my professor of New Testament at Princeton Theological Seminary, was expelled from Nazi Germany in the 1930s for his faith. He left with nothing and found himself destitute in London, England. As he walked the streets, a man suddenly came up to him, handed him a note and vanished. Written on the note were the words, "Call this number." When Otto called, the voice on the other end was that of the principal of a theological faculty offering him a job. Professor Piper told me that the man on the street was an angel who made a supernatural connection for him that radically changed his life and future.

I myself have never seen an angel, although people occasionally report their presence as I speak and minister. However, I have had two remarkable experiences that make me suspect they helped me. In the first case, an approaching car that was within a second or two of hitting me head-on was suddenly knocked out of the way. In the second case, an approaching truck was knocked out of the way. It was as if someone had shoved these vehicles into the next lane.

Was this the work of guardian angels? I don't know for sure. Jesus tells us that each child has an angel watching over him or her: "See that you do not look down on one of these little ones. For I tell you that their angels in heaven always see the face of my Father in heaven" (Matt. 18:10). We are that connected to the Father's presence. It just may be that they will intervene on our behalf in a crisis. They certainly did so for the Early Church in the book of Acts.

Occasionally, I will ask my audiences how many of them have seen an angel. Usually 5 to 10 percent of the people in the crowd raise their hands (at the Azusa Street Celebration of the Pentecostal revival in May 2006, it was more than 50 percent). To be sure, this is anecdotal evidence, but it does force us to ask whether or not our secular worldview has strained out angelic visits.

PROPHECY

A third manifestation of the Spirit is the gift of prophecy. The earliest Christians did not have the New Testament—the apostles and their disciples were just beginning to write and collect it. Most of them also had little of the Old Testament. However, what they did have were individuals who accompanied Jesus throughout His ministry and were eyewitnesses to His resurrection. They memorized Holy Spirit-inspired oral tradition that they received from Jesus and began to write it down.

The earliest Christians also had God's living prophetic voice. As we have seen, on the Day of Pentecost, Peter cites the prophet Joel: "In the last days, God says, I will pour out my Spirit on all people. Your sons and daughters will prophesy" (Acts 2:17). The "Jesus Movement," then, was prophetically driven. Clearly, the apostles execute a prophetic ministry, announcing God's Word in the midst of the people, bringing salvation and healing. According to one definition of prophecy, they "forth-tell," speaking into the present moment.

As an example of this "forth telling," after Peter preaches, his hearers are "cut to the heart" and cry out, "Brothers, what shall we do?" (Acts 2:37). Peter replies, "Repent and be baptized every one of you, in the name of Jesus Christ for the forgiveness of your sins. And you will receive the gift of the Holy Spirit" (v. 38). As with the Old Testament prophets, John the Baptist and Jesus Himself, Peter speaks the word of repentance into the crowd and promises them the gift of the Spirit. All of this is prophetic. As Peter speaks an inspired and empowered word, 3,000 new believers are added to the Church that day (see v. 41).

Beyond prophetic preaching in the Early Church, prophets with words that not only forth-tell but also foretell soon appear. This is the predictive element of prophecy that makes true prophecy so famous and false prophecy so discredited. Luke reports that prophets come from Jerusalem to Antioch: "One of them, named Agabus, stood up and through the Spirit predicted that a severe famine would spread over the entire Roman world" (Luke 11:28). The Church responds by sending financial aid to Jerusalem. Later, as prophets and teachers in Antioch worship and fast, the Holy Spirit speaks to them and says, "Set apart for me Barnabas and Saul for the work to which I have called them." They lay hands on Barnabas and Saul (for commissioning) and send them off (see 13:2-3).

At the end of Paul's third missionary journey, when he decides to return to Jerusalem, he reports to the Ephesian elders, "I only know that in every city the Holy Spirit warns me that prison and hardships are facing me" (20:23). When Paul reaches Caesarea, he stays with Philip the evangelist who has four "unmarried daughters who prophesied" (21:8-9). The prophet Agabus, who previously predicted the famine, then arrives from Judea. Luke recounts:

Coming over to us, he took Paul's belt, tied his own hands
and feet with it and said, "The Holy Spirit says, 'In this way
the Jews of Jerusalem will bind the owner of this belt and
will hand him over to the Gentiles.'" When we heard this,
we and the people there pleaded with Paul not to go up to
Jerusalem. Then Paul answered, "Why are you weeping and
breaking my heart? I am ready not only to be bound, but
also to die in Jerusalem for the name of the Lord Jesus."
When he would not be dissuaded, we gave up and said,
"The Lord's will be done" (21:11-14).

Later, this prophecy is graphically fulfilled. "The whole city
[Jerusalem] was aroused, and the people came running from all
directions. Seizing Paul, they dragged him from the temple. . . . The
[Roman] commander came up and arrested him and ordered him
to be bound with two chains" (vv. 30-33).

While the reigning Lord uses His Spirit and His gifts to speak
to His followers, He can also intervene directly from heaven. When
Saul [Paul] is converted, Jesus asks, "Saul, Saul, why do you persecute me?" Saul responds, "Who are you, Lord?" Jesus replies, "I am
Jesus, whom you are persecuting." Then Jesus gives him a prophetic word: "Now, get up and go into the city, and you will be told what
you must do" (Acts 9:4-6). This unique encounter makes Paul an
eyewitness to the risen Lord and qualifies him to be an apostle (see
1 Cor. 9:1; 15:8; Galatians 1:1,15-16). Later in Revelation, John sees
the reigning Lord and falls at His feet (see Rev.1:17). This inaugurates the vast visions of this fully prophetic book: "The revelation
of Jesus Christ, which God gave him to show his servants what
must soon take place" (Rev. 1:1).

What was then is also now. John Wimber built the Vineyard
based on prophetic direction. At a critical turning point in his life,

the Lord told him, "I've seen your ministry. now I'm going to show you mine."[1] During these early stages, John was asked to meet a woman who claimed to have a word from the Lord for him. John avoided her as long as possible. When they finally met, the woman said nothing. All she did was weep. Exasperated, John demanded that she give him whatever word she had from the Lord. She replied, "That's it." What John received was Jesus weeping over His Church. It was as if he had received a fist to his solar plexus.[2]

In my own situation, after I was fired as the pastor of Mt. Soledad Presbyterian Church, I sank into deep depression. All of my hopes to share in the renewal of that denomination had been dashed. Then our friends, Bob and Nancy Hunt, came to pray with my wife, Kathryn, and myself. As Nancy prayed, she had a vision in which she saw me seated in a chair, and "the chains of the [former] church were melting away." It was as if an elephant had jumped off my chest. I was healed of my depression that night.

With six months severance pay, I prayed each morning for the next step for our lives. Hearing nothing, I remembered John Wimber saying that when he wasn't hearing from the Lord, he prayed that God would speak to his wife, Carol. For two weeks, unknown to Kathryn, I prayed that prayer. Then one morning I returned to the house after walking our dog. Kathryn met me at the door with the announcement, "While I was in the kitchen, God spoke to me. We are to go into the Vineyard." My prayer had been answered.

We called the Wimbers immediately, and they came to our house the next day. John then told me that for the past two years, they had been receiving prophecies in their church that we would be coming into the Vineyard. "But the Lord hasn't released me to tell you this until now," John added. Later that night, Nancy prayed for me and shared the rest of her vision. She said that as I was seated on a platform with the chains of the church melting away, she saw John

Wimber sitting next to me. This new turn in our lives had now been confirmed in three unrelated ways. Kathryn and I forged ahead.

VISIONS AND DREAMS

Because Jesus is the risen Lord who directs His Church and because the Spirit is released, God uses visions and dreams to speak to His followers as well. Again, as He promised through the prophet Joel, "I will pour out my Spirit on all people . . . your young men will see visions, your old men will dream dreams" (Acts 2:17). Visions and dreams become means of grace.

Stephen, the first Christian martyr, received a vision of the reigning Lord as he died: "But Stephen, full of the Holy Spirit, looked up to heaven and saw the glory of God, and Jesus standing at the right hand of God. 'Look,' he said, 'I see heaven open and the Son of Man standing at the right hand of God.' At this they [his executioners] covered their ears and, yelling at the top of their voices, they all rushed him, dragged him out of the city and began to stone him" (Acts 7:55-58). Later, Ananias, a disciple living in Damascus, received direction to pray for Saul after the risen Lord blinded him:

> The Lord called to him in a vision, "Ananias!" "Yes, Lord," he answered. The Lord told him, "Go to the house of Judas on Straight Street and ask for a man from Tarsus named Saul, for he is praying. In a vision he has seen a man named Ananias come and place his hands on him to restore his sight" (Acts 9:10-12).

While Ananias was not thrilled with his assignment, he went. Paul was healed, filled with the Spirit and baptized (see vv. 17-19).

When the angel visited the Roman officer Cornelius, he did so through a vision: "One day at about three in the afternoon he had a vision" (Acts 10:3). The angel commanded Cornelius to send men to find Peter. Likewise, Peter had a trance-like vision concerning unclean animals (symbolizing Gentiles) in which he dialogued with the Lord (see vv. 9-18). As Peter pondered the experience, "the Spirit said to him, 'Simon, three men are looking for you'" (v. 19). The upshot of all of this was that the first Gentile convert was made through angelic, visionary and prophetically directed ministry, which was confirmed when the Holy Spirit fell on Cornelius's household, just as He fell on the Jewish believers in the Upper Room on the Day of Pentecost.

Later, the Holy Spirit prevented Paul from preaching the gospel in the province of Asia by redirecting his mission through a vision: "During the night Paul had a vision of a man of Macedonia standing and begging him, 'Come over to Macedonia and help us.' After Paul had seen the vision, we got ready at once to leave for Macedonia, concluding that God had called us to preach the gospel to them" (Acts 16:9-10). This event opened up the evangelization of Europe through Paul and his companions. During one of Paul's later travels, when he was under duress in Corinth, he also received divine guidance through a vision: "One night the Lord spoke to Paul in a vision: 'Do not be afraid; keep on speaking, do not be silent. For I am with you, and no one is going to attack and harm you, because I have many people in this city.' So Paul stayed for a year and a half, teaching them the word of God" (18:9-11).

As it was then, so it is now. Prophetic visions drove the famous Welsh Revival of 1904. The key leader, Evan Roberts, received a series of visions predicting its course. Regarding these visions, Eifion Evans writes:

There was no question in his [Roberts's] mind as to their authenticity or authority. They were given in conformity to the biblical pattern (Joel 2:28, "your young men shall see visions"), and their message was consistent with biblical truth.

One vision spoke to him of the awful reality of hell. In it he saw a yawning chasm in the form of a fiery, bottomless pit . . . For those in the pit it was a place of torment, and all had entered by the solitary door. A voice spoke to him, "You too would be in their midst apart from God's grace." The mention of grace immediately changed the scene. He found himself with his back to the door, and coming down an incline towards him were countless numbers of people, a surging mass stretching away to the horizon with their faces set towards the pit. From sheer anguish of soul . . . he cried with fierce intensity upon God to rescue them. He pleaded that Hell's door should be closed for one year so that they might have an opportunity to repent. The impression left by this vision remained on his soul for a long time, and the revivalist often referred to it with the profoundest feeling in his public ministry, thankful to God for the respite provided by the revival to so many in answer to his prayer. [In fact, as in the vision, the revival lasted for one year.][3]

At another time, while walking in a garden, Roberts saw a face "full of scorn, hatred and derision, and heard a laugh of defiance." Evans states:

It was the Prince of this world. . . . Then there suddenly appeared another figure, gloriously arrayed in white, bearing in hand a flaming sword borne aloft. The sword fell [on] the first figure, and it instantly disappeared. . . . The message was immediately evident: The Church of Christ was to be triumphant. . . . When the flames of the revival were thoroughly kindled, he referred to it as being the vindication of . . . the vision's validity and divinity.[4]

Evans then comments, "Each vision was presented in biblical categories such as the victory of Christ's kingdom, the spiritual conflict with Satan and the power of God in salvation. They were also prophetic in nature, because each found in the subsequent revival which spread not only over Wales but also across the world, its literal and complete fulfillment. However, although their details were startling and their meaning unmistakable, Roberts dared not act until the way had become clear."[5]

My visionary experience was much less dramatic but no less real than Roberts's. After our Vineyard church's lease expired, we were forced to move. We had no idea where our new location should be. One Friday at the end of a pastors' conference, John Wimber invited the Holy Spirit to come. I suddenly felt sorrow in my spirit, and I bent over, sobbing. I then experienced a vision. It was as if a video-cassette began to play in my brain. For about 20 minutes, I was taken to the area around our house, up and down the streets, across the high school campus, down to the beach, and back to the streets. While I was watching, a great grief gripped me. I knew that it was the Lord's heart, not mine. The video player then stopped.

At that time, our church was located about eight miles north of where Kathryn and I lived. Within a few weeks, the principal of the elementary school near our home, who had previously refused to open his auditorium on Sundays, reversed his decision. We moved the church into the school auditorium—which was a few blocks away from where the tape in my brain had played! Within a year, the Assemblies of God congregation nearby offered their church building for us to use. The building was right in the center of my vision.

A whole new era of ministry opened as we reached out to this community. We moved ahead, totally confident that God was leading us. My gut-wrenching experience would return from time to time as I prayed and the Lord shared His broken heart with me for our community.

SIGNS AND WONDERS

Through the power of the Holy Spirit, Jesus' Kingdom ministry was extended through the Early Church. As Jesus was the Word/Worker, so were His followers. Because they preached the Kingdom, healed the sick and cast out demons during the Lord's earthly ministry, we would expect them to continue this as they took the gospel to the nations. Again, this was prophetically promised when Peter cited Joel's prophecy: "I will show wonders in the heaven above and signs on the earth below . . . before the coming of the great and glorious day of the Lord. And everyone who calls on the name of the Lord will be saved" (Acts 2:19-21).

After Peter preached to the crowd on the Day of Pentecost and many were saved, signs and wonders immediately extended the Kingdom: "Everyone was filled with awe, and many wonders and miraculous signs were done by the apostles" (v. 43). Luke immediately documents some of these signs and wonders when Peter and John approach a cripple who begs at the Temple gate. "When he [the cripple] saw Peter and John about to enter, he asked them for money. . . . Peter said, 'Silver or gold I do not have, but what I have I give you. In the name of Jesus Christ of Nazareth, walk'" (3:6). With that, Peter grasped the man's hands and "instantly the man's feet and ankles became strong. He jumped to his feet and began to walk. Then he went with them into the temple courts, walking and jumping, and praising God" (vv. 7-8).

Later, the members of the Early Church prayed against the opposition that had begun to be directed against them. They asked Lord to enable them to speak His Word with great boldness and stretch out His hand to heal and perform miraculous signs and wonders (see

Acts 4:29-30). Their prayers were soon answered:

> The apostles performed many miraculous signs and won-
> ders among the people. . . . As a result, people brought the
> sick into the streets and laid them on beds and mats so
> that at least Peter's shadow might fall on some of them as
> he passed by. Crowds gathered also from the towns around
> Jerusalem, bringing their sick and those tormented by evil
> spirits, and all of them were healed (5:12,15-16).

Clearly, Luke saw the apostles recapitulating Jesus' Kingdom
ministry in this new era. Yet it was not only the apostles who performed these signs and wonders as the official representatives of
Jesus, but soon a wider circle of believers also began to continue this
same ministry. For example, Luke writes that Stephen, "a man full
of God's grace and power, did great wonders and miraculous signs
among the people" (Acts 6:8). Philip the evangelist also performed
signs and wonders in Samaria: "When the crowds heard Philip and
saw the miraculous signs he did, they all paid close attention to
what he said. With shrieks, evil spirits came out of many, and many
paralytics and cripples were healed" (8:6-8). And Ananias was used
by the Lord to heal Paul in Damascus (see 9:17-19).

The narrative of Acts continues with Peter healing a paralytic
and raising Tabitha (Dorcas) from the dead (see 9:32-43) before
Paul becomes the central figure for the second half of the book.
Kingdom ministry continued through him and his companions in
his three missionary journeys. On Cyprus, Paul blinded the sorcer-
er Elymas with a word of judgment (see 13:11). In Iconium, Paul
and Barnabas spoke boldly for the Lord, who confirmed their message by enabling them to do signs and wonders (see 14:3). In Lystra,
a crippled man who was lame from birth was healed (see 14:8-10).

Later, in Philippi, Paul and Silas were confronted with a slave girl with a spirit "by which she predicted the future" (16:16). After the girl harassed them for many days, Paul finally said to the spirit, "In the name of Jesus Christ I command you to come out of her!" At that moment, the spirit left her (see 16:18). In Ephesus, "God did extraordinary miracles through Paul, so that even handkerchiefs and aprons that had touched him were taken to the sick, and their illnesses were cured and the evil spirits left them" (19:11-12). And in Troas, Paul raised Eutychus from the dead (see 20:7-12).

When we discussed Jesus' Kingdom ministry earlier, we argued that signs and wonders weren't simply given to document that Jesus was the Son of God or to provide the apostles with credentials as His representatives on Earth. Instead, for the Kingdom to be within reach, the lost must be converted, the sick must be healed, and the demonized must be delivered. Otherwise, the inbreaking of God's Kingdom rule becomes abstract and people are left in bondage.

To push miracles into the upper story of good theology, to make them out as symbols of an ideal spiritual state or, worse, to see them as a primitive ("mythological") way of explaining natural events undermines the foundation of New Testament faith. Even the postmodern shift to subjectivity and relativism that states that the miracle is in us and is simply our perception (not "out there" in time, space and history) is no help. Either Satan's kingdom is being overcome, or it isn't. Either God's kingdom is breaking in, or it isn't. Either Jesus is the King, or He isn't. There is no neutral ground. History can't be reduced to our own mindset or limited experience.

We live in the midst of the Kingdom come and coming. God's Kingdom assaults Satan's counterfeit kingdom, setting the captives free and restoring the goodness of God's creation. Yet God's Kingdom power is released in the midst of suffering and persecution. To this we now turn.

CHAPTER 17

PERSECUTION IN THE KINGDOM

The book of Acts, like the Gospels, records not only Kingdom power but also Kingdom suffering. Jesus, the Davidic Warrior-King who brings the Kingdom within reach, is also the Suffering Servant who was rejected, shamed and abandoned on the cross as He bore away our sins. In the book of Acts, His followers live out this double reality. They minister in the power of the Kingdom come and experience the backlash of undermining Satan's grip on the kingdoms of this world. How does this unfold?

First, as Jesus did before them, those in the Church progressively liberated Jews from the legal, cultic and territorial religion centered in Torah, Temple and the Land. As with the launch of Jesus' ministry, the Church experienced initial popularity: "They broke bread in their homes and ate together with glad and sincere hearts, praising God and enjoying the favor of all the people" (Acts 2:46-47). But this warm reception didn't last long.

PERSECUTION BY JEWISH AUTHORITIES

After Peter healed the crippled beggar outside of the Temple—providing him with the opportunity to preach Jesus in the Temple—opposition set in. The priests, the captain of the Temple guard and the Sadducees arrested Peter and John "because the apostles were teaching the people and proclaiming in Jesus the resurrection of the dead" (Acts 4:2). Not only did the Sadducees oppose the resurrection in general and the claim of Jesus' resurrection in particular, they were also threatened by the success of the Early Church. Luke records that the number of male converts at this time reached about 5,000—a number that is easily doubled when women are included. Clearly, Jerusalem was shaken.

The apostles now faced the same court that condemned Jesus. However, because of their popularity, they were simply warned by the authorities to cease and desist preaching the gospel (see v. 21). Later, they were again arrested and, as we have seen, miraculously released by an angel (see 5:19). The apostles immediately returned to the Temple to preach, where they were arrested again (see vv. 25-26). As before, the religious leaders commanded the apostles not to teach in Jesus' name, flogged them, and then released them (see v. 40) But Luke concludes:

> The apostles left the Sanhedrin [court], rejoicing because they had been counted worthy of suffering disgrace for the Name [of Jesus]. Day after day, in the temple courts and from house to house, they never stopped teaching and proclaiming the good news that Jesus is the Christ (vv. 41-42).

Notice the double theme here that we traced in Mark: The apostles experience joy in suffering. This is our life now between the times, the Kingdom come and coming.

With Stephen's martyrdom in Acts 7:54-60, the persecution intensified. As a result, the Jerusalem church became scattered "throughout Judea and Samaria" (8:1). This lead to the evangelization of the Samaritans and the conversion of the Ethiopian eunuch; and Saul, the High Priest's agent, attempts to persecute the Christians in Damascus (see 8:4-8,26-40; 9:1-2). However, as Saul traveled along the road to Damascus, he was confronted by the risen Lord and decided to follow Christ. The mission to the Gentiles, opened through Peter, will now gradually shift to Saul (now known as Paul), the apostle to the Gentile world.

Although Paul continued Kingdom ministry in Kingdom power, he too soon suffered persecution. For example, in Lystra, after Paul healed a man lame from birth, the crowd declared Barnabas to be the god Zeus and Paul to be Hermes. Pagan priests were ready to sacrifice animals to them, but Paul rejected this absurdity and preached the living God, the Creator of all things. Then Jews from Antioch and Iconium arrived, attacked Paul, won over the crowd and stoned him, leaving him for dead (see 14:8-19).

Recovering miraculously, Paul gathered converts in Derbe and retraced his steps, "strengthening the disciples and encouraging them to remain true to the faith. 'We must go through many hardships to enter the kingdom of God,' they said" (v. 22). Here we have it again: Kingdom power and Kingdom suffering. Both always appear at the intersection of this present evil age and the age to come.

PERSECUTION BY ROME

For a season, the new Christian movement was covered by the Roman toleration of the Jews. But as the Church begins to gain Gentile converts and is rejected by the Jews, this fades away. N. T. Wright observed that just as Jesus subverted the Temple, so too the Church subverted the Empire.[1] In the same way that the Jerusalem Church confronted the Jewish authorities, the Gentile mission now confronted the Roman authorities.

Although Paul clearly had great success among the Gentiles, he also suffered at the hand of Rome. In Philippi, after he delivered a demonized girl, her handlers charged, "These men are Jews, and are throwing our city into an uproar by advocating customs unlawful for us Romans to accept or practice" (Acts 16:20-21). Paul and his companion, Silas, were stripped, beaten and jailed by the magistrates (see 16:22-23). When Paul identified himself as a Roman citizen, he and Silas were released and asked to leave the city.

The incident repeated itself in Thessalonica, where Paul's opponents charge, "They are all defying Caesar's decrees, saying that there is another king, one called Jesus" (17:7). This threw the crowd and city officials into turmoil. Paul and Silas slipped away to Berea, where they were pursued by their Jewish antagonists (see v. 13). Paul then moved on to Athens and Corinth. There, the Jews again provoked trouble, but Gallio, proconsul of Achaia, saw the conflict as intra-Jewish and removed himself from the dispute (see 18:1-16).

After a substantial stay in Corinth, Paul moved on to Ephesus, where many people involved in magic arts converted to the faith and burned their paraphernalia. Silversmiths in the city, however, saw the new faith as an attack on their images of Artemis, the Ephesian goddess (see 19:23-27). A riot broke out, and Paul departed. He then made a swing through Macedonia and Greece, returned to Asia, and journeyed to Jerusalem, where prophecies of his coming arrest were fulfilled (see 20–21). Finally, after much suffering—and with an appeal to Caesar himself—Paul was shipped to Rome. Luke closes his narrative of Acts with Paul under house arrest in Rome, witnessing to Jewish leaders. As the curtain drops, Luke reports, "Boldly and without hindrance he [Paul] preached the kingdom of God and taught about the Lord Jesus Christ" (28:31).

Both the Gospel of Luke and the book of Acts reveal the dynamic of the Kingdom come on Earth as it is in heaven and the counter thrust against that Kingdom. As we have seen, opposition to the Kingdom comes from both Jews and Gentiles. It is powered in Judaism by allegiance to the Temple and the Law and in the Roman

Empire by allegiance to pagan idols and their cults. In both cases, the gospel subverts and transforms the world. In both cases, the Spirit's power is released and the assaults of the enemy are endured. By God's miracle, suffering becomes redemptive and the Kingdom, like a small seed planted, begins to grow for a great harvest. Christianity, at its purest, is a revivalist movement. Tested by suffering, it "raises" the dead.

THE CONTINUING STORY

We have little space here to recount how Rome sought to stamp out the Early Christians. The Church father Tertullian wrote famously that the blood of the martyrs was the seed of the Church.[2] As reported, the Early Christians outlived and outlasted the pagans. Power evangelism was joined with power suffering.

On the way to his impending death in a Roman arena, Ignatius of Antioch, an early-second-century bishop, wrote to the Romans:

> This is the first stage of my discipleship; and no power, visible or invisible, must grudge my coming to Jesus Christ. Fire, cross, beast-fighting, hacking and quartering, splintering of bone and mangling of limb, even the pulverizing of my entire body—let every horrid and diabolical torment come upon me, provided only that I can win my way to Jesus Christ! . . . to die in Jesus Christ is better than to be monarch of earth's widest bounds. He who died for us is all that I seek; He who rose again for us is my whole desire.[3]

Justin Martyr, in the later second century, also writes:

> It is clear that, although beheaded, and crucified, and thrown to wild beasts . . . and fire, and all other kinds of torture, we do not give up our confession. But the more such things

happen, the more do other persons and in larger numbers become faithful believers and worshippers of God through the name of Jesus.[4]

Fast forward again to the eighteenth century. As John Wesley evangelized England, he also engaged in spiritual warfare and suffered accordingly. One time, a group tried to drown him out while he was preaching. Wesley writes, "I turned on them immediately, and offered them deliverance from their hard master [the devil]. The word sunk deep into them, and they opened not their mouth. Satan, thy kingdom hath suffered loss. Thou fool! How long wilt thou contend with Him that is mightier than thou?"[5] Another time, Wesley suffered a more direct assault: "While I was preaching in Long-Lane, the host of the aliens gathered together: And one large stone (many of which they threw) went just over my shoulder. But no one was hurt in any degree: For thy 'kingdom ruleth over all.'"[6] And later, as he preached in a field, mockers tried to drive a herd of cows through the crowd. Then they threw a shower of stones, one of which struck Wesley just between the eyes. He writes:

> But I felt no pain at all; and, when I had wiped away the blood, went on testifying with a loud voice, that God hath given to them that believe, "not the spirit of fear, but of power, and of love, and of a sound mind." And by the spirit which now appeared through the whole congregation, I plainly saw what a blessing it is when it is given us, even in the lowest degree, to suffer for his name's sake.[7]

Reflect for a moment on how amazing this is: Wesley is hit by a rock and is bleeding. However, rather than running for shelter, he continues his sermon, and the attitude of the crowd soon changes in his favor. Just as Peter and Paul could not be kept down, so too no one could stop this man.

In our own era, the Chinese Church is an example of a bloodied yet joyous church. Let's return to Brother Yun and the house church movement. Yun and his bride, Deling, were brought together through the efforts of their matchmaking mothers. When Yun met his wife-to-be, he told her, "God has chosen me to be His witness and to follow Him through great hardships and the way of the cross. I don't have any money and am always being pursued by the authorities. Do you really want to marry me?" Deling answered, "Don't worry, I will never let you down. I will join with you and together we will serve the Lord."[8]

When the couple arrived at the marriage office to sign in, they were immediately separated. Yun recounts, "The clerk had realized that my name was on the Public Security Bureau's 'Wanted' list. Several officers came and arrested me. This was the beginning of our life together."[9] Yun's wife adds, "Three or four months after we were married, we were together in a meeting about 30 kilometers from our home. Yun had been arrested but managed to escape from custody, so from that time he became a wanted man and was unable to return home. He therefore went on the run, preaching the gospel all over China."[10]

Yun himself described his career as "fleeing evangelism."[11] In July of 1981, he was arrested again while leading a meeting of 120 house church believers. He recounts, "As the police car drove me to the station the [tire] deflated and I was able to escape. . . . That night as I lay down on the wet ground I cried out to God, 'Why are they treating us like this? Why can't you protect us?'" Then Yun remembered, "To this you were called, because Christ suffered for you, leaving you an example, that you should follow in his steps."[12]

Yun concludes, "We must submit ourselves to God and embrace whatever he allows to happen. Sometimes there are times of peace, other times struggle and persecution. But both are from the

Lord, to mould us into the vessels he wants us to be."[13] He adds, "Suffering, persecution and imprisonment made his [Christ's] gospel rapidly spread throughout China. If our lives had been more comfortable we'd probably have stayed in our home villages. But because we were always fleeing to new places the gospel spread to many areas that had never heard it."[14] Yun's account here is just the beginning of unimaginable suffering that he would endure for the gospel. His whole story was one of blood— the blood of the Cross and his own blood that stained the roads and prisons of China as the gospel proceeded through him and the suffering churches.

CONCLUSION

What we see here is the Early Church in revival, recapitulating not only the power ministry but also the power suffering of her Lord. The Kingdom, inaugurated in Jesus' earthly life, atoning death, resurrection, ascension and reign, now expands with the same kind of power He released and the suffering He endured. The generations to follow, especially those on the cutting edge of evangelism, are marked the same way. We enter the Kingdom through the gate marked "Kingdom Power/Kingdom Suffering." As we do so, we can pray this prayer:

Lord Jesus,
give me the power to do Your works
and the grace to experience Your suffering.
However it may come,
hold me through the hour of trial
and show me Your compassionate face.
Amen.

But what kind of a community does the Kingdom produce? How can it become an instrument of the Kingdom? To this we now turn.

CHAPTER 18

COMMUNITY OF THE KING

In his book *Bradshaw on the Family,* author John Bradshaw estimates that most of us come from dysfunctional families that don't work in a healthy way.[1] In fact, all of us come from dysfunctional families! How do I know? Because of original sin. We have all inherited the brokenness of past generations and are continually being molded by this fallen world order. Then we add our own sin to the mix (see Eph. 2:1-3). Conversion starts the healing process that will go on for a lifetime and will be completed "face to face" (see 1 Cor. 13:12).

Sadly, when many of us become Christ followers, we act out our dysfunctional family issues in the church. Anne Wilson Schaef says that all who are in the helping professions—including priests and pastors—are "untreated codependents."[2] As an addict is addicted to drugs, so they are addicted to people. Codependent people find their identity and value on the outside rather than on the inside. They constantly need others to affirm them. They are the classic "people pleasers."

Church work tends to be the perfect place for these individuals to live out this sickness. For instance, most pastors praise the Lord when people tell them that they wait breathlessly for their next sermon and that they couldn't get through the week without their Sunday "spiritual fix." Because pastors need the flock to tell them who they are, they are unable to hold people accountable, exercise discipline, correct their theology or exhort others about their behavior. Codependent people live shame-based lives and are scared to death of abandonment or rejection. A hostile encounter often exposes this and becomes a "death experience" for the person.

Rafael Sanchez, former Executive of the San Diego Presbytery, told me that he didn't know one Presbyterian minister who had a healthy relationship with his father. Think what this does for their sense of masculine self. They want the church to be for them what their father never was. Because this is impossible, they become angry at the congregation for not meeting their dependency needs. Sick themselves, they make the church sicker still.

Because we are wounded in community (with this fallen world order producing dysfunctional families and churches), we will only get healed in community. When the King is present and the Kingdom within reach, the Church will emerge as a healthy instrument of His kingdom. The real gospel will birth a community that is getting well.

What does this look like? Paul gives us his answer in Ephesians 4 and 5 by demonstrating how the risen Lord gifted His church with apostles, prophets, evangelists and pastor-teachers (or teaching pastors). These seminal gifts reveal God's organizational structure, or business plan. Yet these are not offices to be filled; they are gifts to be received. Christ calls us and anoints us for these ministries, and as we keep our spiritual eyes open, we will spot these gifts as they appear in our midst (or we will pray them into being). Jesus' plan is for the Church to be an instrument of His kingdom and to do Kingdom work.

AN APOSTOLIC CHURCH

First, Paul states that the Church is founded on the apostles. The narrow definition of "apostle" is the Twelve. As we have seen, they were the New Israel, fulfilling the role of Jacob's 12 sons, who in turn fathered the 12 tribes of Old Israel. Now that the final Exodus had arrived, 12 apostles (plus Paul, who was "abnormally born"; see 1 Cor. 15:8) will father the Church.

The apostles, by definition, had to be personally called by Jesus, had to share in His earthly ministry, and had to be eyewitnesses to His resurrection (see Acts 1:22). Discipled by Christ, they learned His teaching and imitated His life, preaching the Kingdom, casting our demons and healing the sick. The very ministry of Jesus was deposited in them. They bore His authoritative Word, guaranteed its authenticity (through the guidance of the Holy Spirit), reinvested that Word in their emerging churches, and recorded His Word in what now makes up our New Testament. Apostles also bore Jesus' authoritative work in character and ministry as signs and wonders displayed the presence of the Kingdom.

The apostles were church planters. They preached the gospel in the power of the Spirit, holding up "Christ crucified" before their hearers. They founded communities by calling their hearers to repent, believe, enter the Kingdom, be baptized (as the sign of their final exodus) and join together as the new people of God.

The Twelve Apostles, plus Paul, are irreplaceable. We can no more add to them than we could add to the 12 sons of Jacob. The Twelve were the foundation of the Church, called to be instruments of the Kingdom. Thus, while there can be no New Testament objection to using the term "apostle" in its wider usage, no living person can replace the unique authority of the Twelve (plus Paul).

The word "apostle" (in the Hebrew behind the Greek) means "One sent with the commission and authority of the sender." The best English equivalent is the word "ambassador," or one who officially represents his or her sending country. Rich Nathan says that a true apostle bears not only the words and works of Jesus but also His wounds. He suffers the onslaught of Satan and the hostility of this world system. He also moves into the pain and suffering of people, bringing Kingdom healing and power to the sick and powerless. The oppressed are then liberated from injustice by the dynamic of God's kingdom overcoming the kingdoms of this world.

Anyone claiming to be an apostle today must pass several biblical tests: Is the person called to the Church by Christ Himself? Is he or she true to the simple gospel of the sheer grace of God given in the death and resurrection of our Lord Jesus Christ? Does he or she bear the apostolic doctrine as revealed in the New Testament and in the early creeds? Does this person plant churches? Does he or she minister the power of the Spirit in signs and wonders? Does this individual suffer for and with Jesus? Is this person self-important or, like Paul, is he or she "the scum of the earth, the refuse of the world"? (1 Cor. 4:13; see also Gal. 1:1-17; 1 Cor. 9:1-2; 15:1-11; Rom. 15:18-20; Eph. 2:20; 4:11).

However we understand this, the Church must be apostolic, founded on the Word and works of Jesus as transmitted to us through His apostles. Apostolic faith will build the Church, confront heresy and immorality, and plant churches in new fields. Remember, the person who bears the apostolic message and ministry bears the apostolic succession. It is a gift that is given, not an office that is filled.

A PROPHETIC CHURCH

As previously mentioned, the earliest Christians had little of the Old Testament and none of the New Testament, which was just being written at the time. In effect, they had none of what we hold to be essential for church planting today. However, what they did have was the word and works of Jesus as transmitted through the apostles and other disciples, bits of the Old Testament, and perhaps a letter from Peter or Paul. They also had the living Word of God, prophetically given and received. Moreover, the earliest Christians had each other—a worshiping community sharing life together in the ministry of the Spirit (see John 14:16-17,26; 15:26-27; 16:7-15).

Prophets emerged quickly in the Early Church, starting on the Day of Pentecost. The Church was prophetically driven—revelation was given through the Spirit to build up its life. In fact, Paul taught that prophecy was the most desirable and important spiritual gift (see 1 Cor. 14:1).

Coming with divine anointing, prophets spoke God's Word into the life of the Church. This living Word brought comfort and conviction. As we have seen, not only was Jesus' ministry prophetically driven, but the ministry of the Early Church was as well.

This is an essential sign that the Kingdom has broken in upon us. The God who spoke for Himself is speaking to us now. We are living in the age of revelation. The new age, promised by Joel, is here. Thus, we must welcome prophets. We must give them time and space. We must allow them to be heard in public gatherings. At the same time, we need to keep in mind that like any other gift, this gift can be abused. So prophets must also submit to the local church body and to each other. All in the church are to discern their messages. Do they come with the anointing of the Holy Spirit? Do they comfort, edify and build up the church? Have they been released by its leaders? Do they have a high degree of accuracy? Is their message consistent with the written Word of God? (The Holy Spirit never contradicts Himself). The Spirit will witness to the whole worshiping community whether a particular prophet is speaking the word of God in their midst.

AN EVANGELISTIC CHURCH

The Church is missional at its core. As evangelists share the gospel, each convert depletes Satan's kingdom by one. As John Wimber stated, this is ground-level spiritual warfare. Evangelists extend God's kingdom throughout this planet that is being redeemed. God promises to bless the nations through father Abraham. People of faith are His true children, and the blessing, now given to the nations, is the promised Holy Spirit Himself, received by faith, transforming and conforming them to Christ together (see Gal. 3:1-14).

Evangelists carry the *evangel*, or the good news. They, too, minister in the power of signs and wonders. They, too, are Spirit-led. They, too, plant churches true to the apostolic faith and incorporate their converts into local bodies of believers. Their gifting is to advance the gospel on the intellectual, spiritual, cultural and geographical frontiers where this age and the age to come intersect.

A NURTURING CHURCH

It is common to speak of the fivefold ministry of apostle, prophet, evangelist, pastor and teacher. This makes up the renewed or restored church. Unfortunately, the Greek grammar only gives us a fourfold ministry. The last seminal gift unites both teaching and pastoring. In other words, teachers are to be pastors.

Teacher-pastors are to both teach and live the apostolic faith by caring for the flock. They are to build up the church by example. They are to exhort as well as instruct. They are to heal as well as save. They are to protect and defend the flock against the enemy and his false teachers that are disguised as "angels of light" (2 Cor. 11:14). They are to nourish, lead and rest the flock. They are to raise up under-shepherds.

Teacher-pastors are called together to a lifetime of care-giving and nurturing others. Paul exhorts the Thessalonians, "Now we ask you, brothers [and sisters], to respect those who work hard among you, who are over you in the Lord and who admonish you. Hold them in the highest regard in love because of their work" (1 Thess. 5:12-13).

AN EQUIPPING CHURCH

God's gifts are given to be given. They are not ends in themselves. Their purpose is to equip the whole Church for ministry. In the words of John Wimber, "Everybody gets to play," and these gifts make this happen.

All too often, we isolate the gifts of apostle, prophet, evangelist and pastor-teacher. We idealize them. We make those who possess these gifts prominent and pay them well. We admire their anointing and support their ministry, but we really don't want them to equip us to minister. We are happy to be passive, sitting in the grandstands, cheering them on as they play the game for us.

In turn, they often enjoy this too. Equipping others is messy and, at times, disappointing. It takes risk, time and energy. It takes the focus off the equipper. It spreads the attention to the whole body, not just the anointed leaders. After all, disciples may become more effective than their leaders. They could become competitive. If they get too good, the leaders could be out of a job.

But the risen Lord calls us out of the grandstands and onto the field to play our unique position. His gifts are not given to entertain us or even to inspire us, but to equip us. Apostles, prophets, evangelists and pastor-teachers are to be "player-coaches." They are to show us how to do ministry and then put us into action. They are to coach us, work with us, condition us, and watch us. As they plant churches, we plant churches. As they receive and speak God's Word, we receive and speak God's Word. As they minister in signs and wonders, we minister in signs and wonders. As they heal the sick and cast out demons, we heal the sick and cast out demons. As they evangelize the lost, we evangelize the lost. As they feed the church, we feed the church. As they love people, we love people. As we learn how to play from them, we become players ourselves—and Jesus' Kingdom ministry is extended through us.

If you are in leadership, ask yourself who you are personally training with the gifts you have received. Are you reproducing your ministry in others' lives? If not, why not?

Clearly, none of us will do all of the above. Each gift releases other gifts to support and extend ministry. This includes intercession, administration, acts of mercy and helping. Much of the body functions through gifts that are not visible or spectacular in nature. However, because Jesus is Lord and head of His Church, through the whole body working together to be apostolic, prophetic, evangelistic and nurturing, we will learn how to play our position and use every gift He releases to us. We will also appreciate the gifts of others (rather than coveting them), bless them and put them into action in ministry.

Frankly, discovering our gifts often comes by trial and error. Some gifts come by stepping out in faith and then receiving confirmation. Some come through the wisdom and affirmation of others in the body. Some come by repeated successes and admitted failures. Some only come with a measure of maturity. Some come with the dynamic of the Spirit when we learn to play new positions (often with great shock and surprise). Some come by prophetic direction.

Some come by persevering prayer. Some come by transferred anointing. Some come by simply feeling, *I'd like to do what he or she does.*

As we live together as brothers and sisters, we will learn our position and learn to play it well. God will put a conviction and passion in our hearts for the ministry He is calling us to. His Spirit will witness to our spirits. Others will affirm our gifting—not out of a codependent need to gain our approval, but out of a genuine appreciation for what God has done through us.

All equipping is for the work of service, or ministry. Ministry is not the territory of a few; it is for the whole Church. It is simply "service"—getting out of ourselves, into others and serving them with the serving heart of Jesus. We do not serve them to use or abuse them, control them or create a sick dependency upon ourselves, but to build them up—to love God and genuinely love and connect with each other.

Through this service, we all will grow up into Christ. Our goal is nothing less than becoming fully like Him: Christians, or Little Christs. God is relentlessly committed to repopulating this planet with images of Himself—starting with you and me! We need to pray for this transformation now!

RADICAL CHANGE

We truly become like that which we worship. Giving up our idols and the addictions they generate means that we leave all of this seduction, emptiness and compulsivity behind. Paul says that when we lost our sensitivity (were unplugged from God), we replaced it with sensuality (see Eph. 4:19). Lust makes us feel alive. Lust drives us—and this drive progressively grows within us. Because we quickly reach tolerance for the objects of our lust (i.e., sex, money, food, power, greed, people), we need more of the same to get the same effect. As

Paul states to the Ephesians, we have a "continual lust for more" (v. 19). This is the short road to addiction, bondage and oblivion.

But God does not leave us in this bondage. In Jesus, He intervened decisively in history. Now, through His Spirit, He intervenes decisively into our hearts, freeing us from our denial, rationalizations and narcissism.

Paul calls us to put off the old life—deceitful as it is. We are to say no to it and put on the new life of righteousness and holiness (see Eph. 4:24). As we do so, the Holy Spirit will keep on renewing us (see Eph. 4:23, which is in the present passive imperative—God does the work). The crisis of conversion moves us into the process of transformation.

As we mentioned, because we got sick in community, we will get well in community. This community is gifted by the risen Lord to be grounded in the apostolic faith. It hears the prophetic and living Word of God, passionately reaches the lost, and builds new believers up relationally (through pastoring) and substantially (through teaching). As this happens, this community will be equipped for ministry and the whole mission, the Jesus Movement, will grow.

What then is to be the quality of our life together? How will we share our lives with each other in healthy ways? We now turn to this.

CHAPTER 19

RELATING IN THE KINGDOM

What does real community look like? What does it mean for us to become whole again? What is the road to becoming more and more like Christ? Practically, how does it work? Paul answers these questions by teaching us how to shape our relationships, become like Jesus, and live together through the power of His Spirit. Remember, we can't do this alone. It's not just "Jesus and me"; it's "Jesus and me and you and us." There is no option. God has created us to work in relationships.

TELL THE TRUTH

Therefore each of you must put off falsehood and speak truthfully to his neighbor, for we are all members of one body.
Ephesians 4:25

In the kingdom of darkness, we were all lied to. Satan is the father of lies (see John 8:44). He lies to us about God, ourselves and the meaning of life. Moreover, because we grew up in dysfunctional families, we were often victims of these lies through the verbal abuse we received. We have been shamed, inflated (flattered) or deflated (assaulted). Many false prophecies have been spoken over us, such as, "You'll never amount to anything."

Because of this, we learned to lie to ourselves (denial) and to each other, and to hide behind false fronts. We fear exposure. We rationalize and justify our attitudes and actions. We mask our selfishness with culture and class or anger and destruction. We become codependent on others and their views of us and of our world. We have let them define our lives.

But when Jesus breaks in and enters our history and our hearts, the lights go on. Now we know who God is, who we are and the purpose of our lives. We learn that we are to love God, ourselves, and our neighbor (and even our enemy) out of a strong sense of identity with him or her—no strings attached. Having had a truth encounter with Jesus, we become truthful with each other. We learn to speak the truth in love to expose the enemy's lies and to build each other up in the community (see Eph. 4:15).

As I write this, a few of my best brothers are meeting this weekend to share the lies they have believed in from childhood and to break the power of those lies in Jesus' name. Their next step is to speak the truth to each other—the truth in Jesus. Will you join with them? Will you commit to no more coverup, no more manipulation, no more defensiveness, no more fear? Will you receive Jesus' truth, listen to His Spirit of truth, bask yourself in God's Word of truth, and start telling the truth?

Jesus promised that His truth would set us free (see John 8:32). Because we belong to the King and to each other, we are now in a community that lives out the truth. The time has passed for putdowns, gossip and salacious attacks. Now we have received the truth and walk in it together. We are a community of the truth—the truth of the Kingdom that commands every area of our life.

DEAL WITH ANGER

"In your anger do not sin": Do not let the sun go down while you are still angry, and do not give the devil a foothold.
Ephesians 4:26-27

Anger is a universal human emotion. We can express it actively by blowing up or passively by isolating ourselves. We are to acknowledge our anger, but we are not to harbor it.

Anger is also a secondary emotion. Behind anger lies fear or pain. When we are attacked, we attack back. When we are in pain, we fight back. But Paul tells us to resolve our anger quickly (before the sun goes down), for if we harbor it, it will eat us alive. Who wants migraine headaches, lower-back pain, arthritis or an endangered immune system?

Has someone hurt you? Deal with it and tell that person the truth. Pray for God's love to empower you. Forgive and release. Don't allow yourself to live in the prison of your unforgiveness. You only hurt and embitter yourself. Moreover, if you harbor anger, you give the devil an opportunity to get a foothold in your life. Many people experience demonic attack or attachment because of past unresolved pain. Because they are unwilling to forgive, they give the devil a legal right, a "place" in their spirits (and bodies), to be there. So as you agree to not let the sun go down on your anger, you effectively close the door to the enemy.

We are a protected community of the Kingdom. The devil has lost his entry point. Confessing anger quickly bars the door to him.

GET A JOB

He who has been stealing must steal no longer, but must work, doing something useful with his own hands, that he may have something to share with those in need.
Ephesians 4:28

We live in an "entitlement" culture. We believe we are entitled to everything. The clever among us have learned how to work the system.

For instance, I know a number of homeless people who prefer to stay on the streets and use Church and government agencies to sustain their lifestyle. They learn how to enjoy their retirement from life and have no inclination to give it up (many other homeless people do want to get off the streets, and we need to go to them and help them start again).

Of course, it's not just the homeless who feed off the system—others among us do it through shady deductions on their income tax returns, charging up irresponsible credit card debt, or inflating the value of their property and possessions ("Whatever the market will bear").

When we come into the community of the King, we begin to take responsibility for our lives and no longer can simply use others. Paul tells us, in effect, that we need to get a job, provide for ourselves and our dependents, and then give the rest away to those who cannot provide for themselves (such as orphans, widows, children, the physically challenged, the addicted and the elderly).

Our goal is to take care of those who are unemployed (or even unemployable) so that they can get a job, take care of themselves and their dependents, and then repeat the cycle by caring for others. This may include providing a living situation and job training and establishing clear disciplines in a loving community. It may also include assisting others to find healing from the ravages of addiction and self-destruction.

Work is not to be drudgery. Work brings dignity. We were created to work—to tend and improve the Garden: "The LORD God took the man and put him in the Garden of Eden to work it and take care of it" (Gen. 2:15). We die to our narcissism and self-consumption as we go to work and do all for the glory of God (see Col. 3:17).

GET INTO OTHERS

Do not let any unwholesome talk come out of your mouths,
but only what is helpful for building others up according to their
needs, that it may benefit those who listen.
Ephesians 4:29

Before Christ claims us, we are self-consumed. Our basic question is, "What's in it for me?" But now, having died to ourselves, we begin to ask, "What's in it for others?"[1] Our narcissism goes daily to the Cross. Thus, Paul says that we are to no longer let "unwholesome talk" spew out of our mouths. We are to forgo criticism, judgment, put-downs and gossip, and learn to care for others.

This begins by learning how to listen to others—not to correct or advise them, but to understand them. The way that we hear is through active listening. Here is a test: If someone tells us something, are we able to tell it back to them in their own words (e.g., "I hear you say that . . .") without adding our personal commentary? This alone is an act of love.

Paul says that we are to speak "only what is helpful for building others up according to their needs, that it may benefit those who listen" (Eph. 4:29). So we need to ask ourselves, *Does what I say really help others, or does what I say hurt them? Does what I say build others up or tear them down? Does what I say meet others' needs or meet my needs as I take over the conversation and use it to talk about myself? Does what I say benefit my listeners or rip off their time, attention and energy? As others listen to me and build me up, do I reciprocate?* As we grow in our love for Jesus and each other, we will begin to answer "yes" to all of the above questions. We will learn how to listen to others—to truly listen, as they have listened to us. What a great new family to belong to!

WELCOME THE HOLY SPIRIT

And do not grieve the Holy Spirit of God, with whom
you were sealed for the day of redemption.
Ephesians 4:30

Paul warns us against grieving the Holy Spirit. Grief comes from rejection. When the Spirit speaks, reveals, exposes, prophesies, convicts, comes in power and releases His gifts, we have the choice to respond or not. When, out of selfishness, the fear of losing control, theological defensiveness, or harboring our sin, we reject Him, He is hurt ("grieved") and will withdraw. After all, He is the *Holy* Spirit, sent to transform us and make us holy like Himself (or "whole," restoring authentic human nature that was perverted by sin).

Listen to what A. W. Tozer says about grieving the Holy Spirit:

> It is time for us to repent, for our transgressions against the blessed Third Person [the Holy Spirit] have been many and much aggravated. We have bitterly mistreated Him in the House of His friends. We have crucified Him in His own temple as they crucified the Eternal Son of God on the hill above Jerusalem. . . . By unworthy thoughts about Him and unfriendly attitudes toward Him we grieved and quenched Him days without end. . . . We can best repent of our neglect by neglecting Him no more. Let us begin to think of Him as One to be worshipped and obeyed. Let us throw open every door and invite Him in. Let us surrender to Him every room in the temple of our hearts and insist that He enter and occupy as Lord and Master within His own dwelling.[2]

When the Holy Spirit began to move on me in power, I knew that I had a choice to make. I could shut down and turn Him off, or I could go with what He was doing. I chose the latter, and as a result I received a flooding of the Spirit, filling me with praise and joy beyond imagination. The Spirit's gift of tongues exploded out of me. Since that day I have had the same choice to make each day: Shall I welcome the Spirit's gifts and allow them to work through me, or shall I shut Him down and turn Him off?

Although I often fail, I realize that I am on a steep learning curve. As I write this section, I have just finished a healing conference in Toronto. Yesterday, I taught on Jesus' Kingdom warfare against Satan's counterfeit kingdom (a basic theme of this book) to several hundred people. At the ministry time, when we prayed for people "up front," the Spirit encouraged me to model praying for the sick by calling someone up to receive prayer for chronic pain.

A young woman responded and came down to the front, where she began to describe a whole list of problems to me, including serious physical pain, numbness on her left side and loss of hearing in one ear. My prayer team joined me and we began to pray. Suddenly, the woman fell to the floor, squinted her eyes shut (refusing to open them) and began to writhe. Clearly, demonic activity was going on. She spoke through clenched teeth, "It happened in the church." She added, "I hate myself. I am so ugly." (She was very beautiful.) We took her to a side room, where she was delivered from demons and healed from the sexual assault that had taken place in a church sanctuary so long ago.

Later, she stood before the crowd, sane, composed and in her right mind. She testified that Jesus had set her free. My teaching on Kingdom warfare had brought a power encounter with her demons, and the congregation saw the battle rage right in front of them. They also heard her witness that the victory had been won. Out of fear (and a bit of chaos), we could have shut all of this down at the outset. But this would have left a woman in pain and unhealed.

In that ministry moment, we listened to the Spirit, went for it, and got more than we bargained for. The authority and power of Jesus set this woman free, just as it had in the Gospels and the book of Acts. Remember Paul's words in Ephesians: "Do not grieve the Holy Spirit of God, with whom you were sealed for the day of redemption." Each day, pray, "Holy Spirit, come in Jesus' name. I welcome Your presence and ask for Your power. Help me to walk in step with You and do what You are doing. For Jesus' sake, Amen."

BE KIND, COMPASSIONATE, FORGIVING

Be kind and compassionate to one another, forgiving each other,
just as in Christ God forgave you.
Ephesians 4:32

We are to be a community in which genuine love with kindness and compassion draw us together into intimacy. This is exactly what this present generation is looking for. So many come from broken homes and are looking for a family that they can belong to and trust. They want to "hang out." Largely uninterested in programs, they are intensely interested in people.

The problem with transparency and honesty, however, is that if we get close enough, we will hurt each other. Our sharp edges will collide. What should we do when this occurs? Paul states that we should forgive each other, just as in Christ God forgave us. Together, we start at the Cross and end at the Cross. In this life, we never get away from the Cross—in fact, we live there.

John Wimber once said that forgiveness is the currency of the Kingdom. Forgiveness makes community possible. It allows us to have transactions with each other, take risks and recover quickly when we are wrong or wronged. Dietrich Bonhoeffer states that the world wants direct relationships—control, ownership and possession. But when we come to Christ, we surrender our direct relationships to Him. Now, we have only indirect relationships, because Jesus stands between us as our Mediator.[3] We receive His forgiveness, which we then give to each other and move on—humbled and more deeply committed and exposed (which breeds more intimacy). Indeed, forgiveness is the currency of the Kingdom, building and growing authentic community and releasing us for Kingdom ministry.

IMITATE GOD AND LIVE IN LOVE

Be imitators of God, therefore, as dearly loved children and live a life of love, just as Christ loved us and gave himself up for us as a fragrant offering and sacrifice to God.
Ephesians 5:1-2

We are made in God's image. We are redeemed to become what we now are—conformed to the image of Christ Himself. We live this out by imitating God. Central to His character and, therefore, ours, is love—not selfish, self-giving love or "need" love, but "gift" love.[4] God's love does not seek value; rather, it creates and invests value. There is no deeper human experience than being loved fully, freely, unconditionally and eternally. As we receive God's love, we then give it away—for to only possess God's love is to lose its power and value.

Paul tells us that we are "deeply loved children." Recall that what the Father said to the Son at His baptism He also says to us in Him: "You are my Son whom I love; with you I am well pleased" (Mark 1:11). To live a life of love, we need to know and experience that we are loved. Our model is Christ, who "loved us and gave himself up for us as a fragrant [acceptable, attractive] offering and sacrifice to God" (Eph. 5:1). To live a life of love is to fulfill the two Great Commandments: to love God and to love each other (see Mark 12:29-31; Luke 10:27-28).

To live a life of love is to be driven by love in all we think, fantasize, feel, decide, say and do. Love covers everything. Love creates the world. Love sustains the world. Love redeems the world. Love will transform and perfect the world. Love draws us into the love relationships of the Triune God and draws us to each other. After faith turns to sight and hope is fulfilled, only love endures (see 1 Cor. 13:8-13). We must abide in love. It is the greatest of all things!

PURSUE SEXUAL PURITY

But among you there must not be even a hint of sexual immorality, or of any kind of impurity, or of greed, because these are improper for God's holy people. Nor should there be obscenity, foolish talk or coarse joking, which are out of place, but rather thanksgiving. For of this you can be sure: No immoral, impure or greedy person—such a man is an idolater—has any inheritance in the kingdom of Christ and of God.

Ephesians 5:3-5

Our sex drive is a basic instinct. Created by God and blessed by God, we are sexual beings, made to become creators with the Creator as we reproduce the race and find pleasure and fulfillment in a permanent, heterosexual, monogamous union (see Gen. 2:24). Unfortunately, after the Fall, our sex drive, like all our other drives, became perverted and fallen.

We all know how destructive our sex drives can be. Our erotic culture is saturated with sexual exploitation and brokenness. This is the "pornographic generation," in which every imaginable sex act is immediately available in our homes and offices through the Internet. As Jamie Wilson remarked, "Where our eyes go, our feet follow."[5] Rape, incest, adultery, and all kinds of fornication and perversity clog our lives. In fact, it has been estimated that 20 percent of all boys and 30 to 40 percent of all girls are sexually abused in childhood.[6] Sexually transmitted diseases leave millions dead, dying or permanently disabled. But God delivers us from this darkness, forgives us, and begins to heal us and even reprogram our damaged brains.

Our new Christian family is to be sexually safe. Seduction, sexual aggression and violence have no place among us. We repent of our pornographic imaginations and identify the triggers (such as the bar scene, excessive drugs or alcohol, erotic environments, the Internet, depression, sexual insecurity and personal loneliness) that will lead us to act out. We ask Jesus to heal the pain inside, and rather than beating ourselves up, we receive His forgiveness and make a new beginning.

The earliest Christians brought their sexual brokenness into the Church. The Corinthians falsely celebrated the incestuous relationship of a man with his mother-in-law as a sign of Christian freedom (see 1 Cor. 5:1). Others continued to visit prostitutes (see 1 Cor. 6:15-16). Still others became celibate in their marriages (see 1 Cor. 7:5). Paul told them, "Do not be deceived. Neither the sexually immoral nor idolaters nor adulterers nor male prostitutes nor homosexual offenders nor thieves nor the greedy nor drunkards nor slanderers will inherit the kingdom of God. And that is what some of you were" (1 Cor. 6:9-11).

Think about it: The Corinthian Church included adulterers, male prostitutes and homosexuals. How would you like to have these people in your small group or home fellowship? How would you like your family to be exposed to them? But Jesus redeemed their sexual brokenness, as He redeems ours.

Paul tells us, "But among you there must not even be a hint of sexual immorality, or of any kind of impurity, or of greed, because these are improper for God's holy people" (Eph. 5:3). Moreover, our erotic environments must be cleansed: "Nor should there be obscenity, foolish talk or coarse joking, which are out of place, but rather thanksgiving" (Eph. 5:4). These things are now out of place because they devalue the beauty and mystery of our sexuality, cheapen us and reduce us to the exploited sexual objects of our consumer culture.

Paul warns, "For of this you can be sure: No immoral, impure or greedy person—such a [one] is an idolater—has any inheritance in the kingdom of Christ and of God" (Eph. 5:5). The power of lust for sex and possessions easily becomes addictive. Our desires become attached to them and we become their prisoners. We think that we can control them, but they end up controlling us. This is functional idolatry, the spiritual component of addiction. To be free, we must repent, detach, grieve our losses and ask the Holy Spirit to fill us and free us to love God and authentically love each other with all that we are.

CONTEND AGAINST THE DARKNESS

For you were once darkness, but now you are light in the Lord. Live as children of light . . . and find out what pleases the Lord. Have nothing to do with the fruitless deeds of darkness, but rather expose them. For it is shameful even to mention what the disobedient do in secret. But everything exposed by the light becomes visible, for it is light that makes everything visible. This is why it is said, "Wake up, O sleeper, rise from the dead, and Christ will shine on you."
Ephesians 5:8-14

We are soldiers of the Kingdom. We are in God's army, warring against Satan's kingdom. As such, Paul tells us that we are "light in the Lord" and that we should "live as children of light."

Not only are we to have "nothing to do with the fruitless deeds of darkness," we are to expose them (see Eph. 5:11). What is done in secret must be brought into the light—and exposure heals. As they say in Alcoholics Anonymous, "You are as sick as your secrets." When we no longer live shame-based lives or try to medicate our pain with sex, drugs or mood-altering activities, the healing power of Jesus (often through hands-on healing prayer) will restore us to sanity and teach us how to live.

As Paul says, Christ shines on us (see Eph. 5:14). He exposes our dark places, our wounds, our hypocrisy and our self-consumption as He shines His grace, His forgiveness and His resurrection life on us, and we come alive. "Wake up, O sleeper, rise from the dead and Christ will shine on you" (Eph. 5:14).

BE FILLED WITH THE SPIRIT

*Do not get drunk on wine, which leads to debauchery. Instead, be
filled with the Spirit. Speak to one another with psalms, hymns,
and spiritual songs. Sing and make music in your heart to the
Lord, always giving thanks to God the Father for everything, in the
name of our Lord Jesus Christ.*
Ephesians 5:18-20

When the apostles were filled with the Spirit at Pentecost, many accused them of being drunk (see Acts 3:13). In this passage, Paul contrasts wine and being filled with the Spirit. As Paul states, unlike being drunk on wine, to be filled with the Spirit means to be emptied of self—to come under the Spirit's control and experience His power.

The verb Paul uses is a present imperative: "Keep on being filled." Actually, in the original Greek, Paul wrote this instruction to the Ephesians in one long sentence (not the several used by modern translators): "Do not get drunk on wine, which leads to debauchery, instead [but] keep on being filled with the Spirit, speaking to one another with psalms, hymns, and spiritual songs, singing and making music in your heart to the Lord, always giving thanks to God the Father for everything, in the name of our Lord Jesus Christ." In other words, Paul is saying that this is to become our lifestyle and, as a result, we become extravagant worshipers.

So, to keep on being filled with the Spirit, we must become worshipers. Our worship is to be addressed to each other and to God. We are to be a community building each other up in worship and, as we do so, the Spirit will keep on filling us up. He loves our worship and visits us with His gifts and power as we engage with Him and with each other. The vehicles of our worship are psalms (prayers and songs from the Old Testament), hymns (poetic, didactic set songs), and spiritual songs (songs spontaneously authored by the Spirit Himself). This certainly may include "singing in the Spirit" or singing in tongues (see 1 Cor. 14:15).

Singing engages us as whole people. It is a physical as well as a spiritual act. Our minds, hearts and bodies respond as we sing. Worship elevates our mood and opens us up to the Spirit who comes as we worship, which then allows His presence, power and gifts to be released. Moreover, as we sing, we are united to heaven itself where a multitude of angels and the redeemed worship before God's throne. Our imaginations are cleansed and reprogrammed with images of heaven itself. Our hearts are united together as we, the choir, worship before an Audience of One. Worship gets us out of the grandstands as spectators and puts us onto the playing field. All of this is bathed in thanksgiving and rises up to God in the "name [or authority of our Mediator] our Lord Jesus Christ."

SUBMIT

Submit to one another out of reverence for Christ.
Ephesians 5:21

Paul ends his exhortation by calling us to mutually submit to each other. We submit to those who submit to us, and "everybody gets to play." We submit in love. We submit to serve. We humble ourselves before each other. We wash feet. We submit together in advancing the Kingdom into every heart and every place in this dark world that is now coming again under God's sovereign rule. A Christian who is not submitted is a rebellious Christian, filled with fear or arrogance. So ask yourself, To whom are you practically submitted in Christ's Body?

IN SUM

Through his words to the Ephesians, Paul shows how a functional family should work. Rather than continuing to live in dysfunctional families and churches, we learn to tell the truth. We deal with our anger. We close the door to the devil. We take responsibility for our lives and for those in need. We build each other up. We welcome the Holy Spirit. We are kind, compassionate and forgiving as Christ forgives us. We imitate God by living a life of love as Christ loved us. We walk in sexual purity and renounce our idols and addictions. We walk in the light and expose the darkness. We keep on being filled with the Spirit as we worship together and give thanks to God. We submit to each other in love and humility.

This is the community in which we can heal and get well. This is the community that will be the instrument of God's kingdom. It won't just save souls; it will also build lives to be like Jesus. Through this community, marriages, families and economic life will be redeemed (see Eph. 5:21-6:9). This community will fight together against the spiritual darkness that subverts God's good earth, and in turn, it will subvert the world system that tries to subvert it. This is a subversion brought about by love as God's kingdom grows "we know not how" (see Mark 4:26-29). We enter the Kingdom through the gate marked "You Belong to Us; We Belong Together."

We all must hear the Father say, "You are the son [or daughter] I love, in you I am well pleased." We must pray together, "Your kingdom come, Your will be done, on earth, as it is in heaven. Bring Your kingdom now, Lord. Rule again over Your creation, fallen and redeemed. Destroy the devil and all his works. Glorify Yourself as You bring in the new creation, anchored in the resurrection of Your Son. Complete Your Kingdom work. Come, Lord Jesus. Come in triumph. Come in glory. Come to reign. Wipe all the tears from our eyes. Welcome us into the New Jerusalem. Adorn us as Your bride for You, our Bridegroom. For Yours is the kingdom, the power and the glory forever. Amen."

CHAPTER 20

YOU'RE IN THE KINGDOM NOW

The Kingdom is the point of God's agenda. It is the purpose of today's Church. The Church is not an end in itself, however; it is the means to the end of extending the rule and reign of God throughout this planet and, ultimately, throughout the whole universe. Jesus promises that He will build His Church—as a siege army—to knock down the gates of hell (see Matt. 16:18). As the walled city of the enemy falls to this battering ram, billions of captives will be liberated from the dark side.

As we have seen, to come to Christ is to enter His kingdom and be enlisted in His army. In the final exodus, the ultimate Pharaoh, Satan, has his control over us broken, and in the final Passover, Jesus, the Lamb of God, carries away God's wrath. Through this double deliverance, we are now recruited to reclaim the whole creation for the kingdom of God. We no longer believe the lie that we can be "like God" (Gen. 3:5). Delivered from self-worship (our ultimate idolatry and addiction), we are then restored to true worship—the worship of the Triune God.

WORSHIP: THE KEY TO THE KINGDOM

The Great Commandment—to love God with all we are—is first fulfilled in worship. God creates us out of love, and our worship returns our love to Him. This is the ultimate meaning of being made
in His image as male and female. The deepest loss in the Fall was the
loss of worship, but God moved to restore true worship by calling a
special people to Himself.

Worship, as we have seen, is central to our identity and destiny
in the Kingdom. I never tire of quoting N. T. Wright that we become like what (or who) we worship. If we are grateful and thankful subjects of the King, then our deepest joy will be to praise Him
and submit ourselves to Him in love. When we do so, He draws us
intimately into His open heart. The whole of Scripture then
explodes with worship: The heavens declare the glory of God (see
Ps. 19:1) and the morning stars sing to Him together (see Job 38:7).

Wherever Father Abraham moved, he built an altar and worshiped the Lord (see Gen. 12:8; 13:18). After coming out of Egypt,
Moses not only received the Law on Mount Sinai, but he also received
the priesthood, the sacrificial system, and the designs for the Taber-
nacle where the holy God would be properly worshiped and His manifest presence would dwell (see Exod. 20-27). This was the prototype
for Solomon's Temple. At its dedication, the glory of God fell and the
priests could no longer minister; they were physically overwhelmed by
majesty itself (see 1 Kings 8:10-11). Israel's daily worship and annual
festivals were celebrated in the Temple, molding the core of her life.
The book of Psalms, Israel's hymn book, pulsated with worship. And
with the corruption and destruction of the earthly Temple, the
prophets promised a renewed and glorified Temple.

As we have seen, Jesus shifted the Temple functions from
Jerusalem to Himself. Later, Paul taught that the organism of the

Church—the people of God—is the Temple (see Eph. 2:21). Even our bodies, indwelt by the Spirit, are God's temples (see 1 Cor. 6:19). In the book of Revelation, John later stated that one day, when the New Jerusalem comes down from heaven, shining with divine glory, the Lord God Almighty and the Lamb [Jesus] "are its temple" (21:22). There, before the throne of God and of the Lamb, "his servants will serve [a technical term for worship] him. They will see his face, and his name will be on their foreheads . . . the Lord God will give them light. And they will reign for ever and ever" (22:3-5). In the meantime, our worshiping community is united to heavenly worship by the Spirit. We now experience, in part, that day when we will worship before God's throne face to face.

WORSHIP: THE KEY TO THE EARLY CHURCH

Although Paul's epistles show us that worship was the center of the Corinthian church, his letters also show that he had to correct his converts in the way they lived this out (see 1 Cor. 8-14). As Tommy Tyson (a Methodist evangelist and mentor of Francis MacNutt) states, new life is in the nursery, and it is messy.[1] Paul had to spend time correcting these things exactly because they were exploding. Whenever the Spirit is poured out, there will be blessing, some confusion and the enemy's counterattack.

When the Spirit fell on the Toronto Airport Church, millions of people experienced His infilling, gifting and healing. Although some warned of deception, what happened at that church, at its core, was a repetition of Pentecost, with signs and wonders following. The same thing occurred at the Anaheim Vineyard in the early 1980s. For the leaders of that church at the time, it was like pastoring in the midst of a hurricane. Did excesses occur? Of course. But God's power was unleashed and worship took off.

Paul walks a tightrope, then, as he writes to the Corinthians on worship. On the one hand, he doesn't want to quench the Spirit. On the other hand, he wants to order the church. D. Martyn Lloyd-Jones (pastor of Westminster Chapel in London for many years), after warning that we are not to let experience determine Scripture, offers this further warning:

> The second danger, then, is that of being satisfied with something very much less than what is offered in Scripture, and the danger of interpreting Scripture by our experience and reducing its teaching to the level of what we know and experience. . . . In other words, certain people by nature are afraid of the supernatural, of the unusual, of disorder. You can be so afraid of disorder . . . that you become guilty of what the Scripture calls "quenching the Spirit"; and there is no question in my mind that there has been a great deal of this . . . People are so afraid of what they call enthusiasm, and some are so afraid of fanaticism, that in order to avoid those they go right over to the other side without facing what is offered in the New Testament . . . Compare, for instance, what you read about the life of the church at Corinth with typical church life today. "Ah but," you say, "they were guilty of excesses in Corinth." I quite agree. But how many churches do you know at the present time to which it is necessary to write such a letter as the First Epistle of Paul to the Corinthians? Do not put your emphasis entirely on the excesses. Paul corrects the excesses but see what he allows, what he expects. . . . Of course, it is always life that tends to lead to excesses. There is no problem of discipline in a graveyard; there is no problem very much in a formal church. The problem arises when there is life.[2]

Paul's key thesis, then, is that worship needs to build us up rather than tear us down. Consider for a moment how worship wars continue to divide Christians and splinter the Body. Although it is hard to believe today, during the Jesus Movement, even bringing guitars into the Sanctuary sent some traditional Christians packing.

THE ELEMENTS OF WORSHIP

As Paul writes his first letter to the Corinthians, he is highly didactic, polemical and corrective. Because he is addressing particular abuses that were occurring in the Corinthian church, many of our questions go unanswered. We wonder how frequently the church met. Was it scattered in various house churches? Who organized and directed its worship? Did worship simply flow or did it follow the synagogue pattern? How long did the services last? Was there any regular order? What was the relationship between the Lord's Supper and the "charismatic" expression of the Spirit's gifts? How often were unbelievers present? How did the church sing to the Lord? Were there worship leaders? To these and many other questions we have to say, "We just don't know."

Moreover, when Paul addresses local issues that relate to the ancient world, such as eating meat offered to idols, the length of men's and women's hair, wearing veils, the lust of angels, people getting drunk at the Lord's Supper (and getting sick and dying as a result), discrimination against the poor, women interrupting the service with questions, and the abuse of tongues, his teachings are mostly foreign to us. At the same time, because Paul writes under the inspiration of the Holy Spirit, these very chapters are the Word of God. They have enduring value, transcending Corinthian issues. Let's take them in the order of their appearance.

Worship Is Pure

First, our worship is to be pure. In our attempts to be relevant today, we need to be careful that we are not assimilating aspects of the pagan culture into our worship. In his first letter to the Corinthian church, Paul dealt with this issue by answering the question, Can meat, sacrificed to idols in pagan temples, be eaten? Paul responds that because idols are nothing, our freedom is to eat or not to eat. The real question is about caring for our "weaker brother" who is offended by our eating meat with pagan associations or who is tempted to syncretism. Paul concludes, "Therefore, if what I eat causes my brother to fall into sin, I will never eat meat again, so that I will not cause him to fall" (1 Cor. 8:13). As we worship, one eye must be on God and the other must be on our brothers and sisters around us. As we serve God, we also serve each other (see Eph. 5:19). Pure worship cares for both dimensions.

In some liberal and post-modern churches, relativism and syncretism are rampant. We are told that to welcome practicing gay clergy is to be Christlike. We are told that to engage in Transcendental Meditation or yoga is harmless and good for serenity or a flexible body. We are told that the message of God's justice and judgment is psychologically damaging. We are told that to welcome the power of the Spirit in our services is to drive people away. We are told that God doesn't heal today, so it is futile to pray for the sick and give them false expectations. On and on the list goes. But we are Kingdom people, expecting the Kingdom to come as we worship the King. Our focus is on Him, not on our relevance to the culture or to the unsaved.

Worship Is Equal

In addition to pure worship, Paul teaches us that in worship, everybody gets to play. In 1 Corinthians 11:2-16—a difficult and controversial passage—Paul's positive teaching is that the gifts of the Holy

Spirit are given regardless of gender. Unlike the synagogue, women are now fully free to exercise the gifts of the Spirit, of which prophecy is the most precious of them all. Both men and women are to receive and speak God's living Word to the Church and then offer their words back to Him in public prayer (see 1 Cor. 11:4-5).

How the gifts of the Spirit are exercised will depend on our cultural context. But the sovereign Spirit releases us all into ministry: "In the last days, God says, I will pour out my Spirit on all people. Your sons and daughters will prophecy, your young men will see visions, your old men will dream dreams. Even on my servants, both men and women, I will pour out my Spirit in those days, and they will prophesy" (Acts 2:17-18).

Is this going on in your church? If not, at this point, you are sub-biblical.

Worship Is Centered on the Cross

Third, Paul tells us that the Cross is to be central in worship. This is actualized as we celebrate the Lord's Supper together. The broken bread and the poured-out cup proclaim the Lord's death until He returns (see 1 Cor. 11:26). Our meeting together is to humble us, unite us and help us to remember Jesus' death for us. In the sacrament, we also anticipate the day that we will banquet together in the kingdom of God.

The Holy Spirit will move upon us through this sacrament. The way we receive it, the way we search our own hearts, the way we treat each other—all of these are at stake. Although evangelicals especially tend to trivialize this Supper, Paul does not. There is huge power at work here; as we meet Jesus at the Cross, He and His Spirit are present. In the Supper, we will never get beyond this: In the throne-room of God, we will worship the Lamb that was slain (see Rev. 5).

Worship Is Based on Confession

Fourth, true worship has a confessional basis: Together, by His Spirit, we proclaim "Jesus is Lord" (1 Cor. 12:3). To call Jesus "Lord" is to renounce all other lords. To call Jesus "Lord" is to use the Old Testament designation of God Himself. As N. T. Wright shows, Paul puts Jesus as Lord into Israel's fundamental creed: "Hear, O Israel: The Lord our God, the Lord is one" (Deut. 6:4).[3] This is echoed and revised for the Corinthians: "Yet for us there is but one God, the Father . . . and there is but one Lord, Jesus Christ" (1 Cor. 8:6).

Furthermore, to call Jesus "Lord" is to submit once again to His kingdom and His sovereignty. To make this confession could have cost these Christians their lives. Caesar claimed to be "Lord," and he increasingly demanded their worship. But the Early Christians knew that only God is to be worshiped through His Son.

This is the potential price for exclusive worship. Again and again, the Church pays in blood for saying out loud what the Holy Spirit inspires: "Only Jesus is Lord."

Worship Allows the Ministering of Gifts

Fifth, when we meet together in worship, we are all gifted by the Spirit to minister to each other. As we mentioned, these gifts (such as prophecy, words of wisdom and knowledge, tongues, interpretation of tongues, healings and miracles) are not restricted to gender or class. The Spirit gifts these to each of us sovereignly. Thus, all, as inspired by the Spirit, are to speak the living Word of God, respond in faith and minister to each other. Paul writes, "Now to each one the manifestation of the Spirit is given for the common good. To one there is given through the Spirit the message of wisdom, to another the message of knowledge" (1 Cor. 12:7-8).

Do we look for the gifting in each other? Are we ready to receive whatever the Spirit brings? This is the road away from pastor burnout. This is the way to rid the Church of professionalism and restore ministry to the whole community. This is the way for leaders to surrender their control issues to the Lord and to the Church. Are we willing to risk it and create an environment in which Spirit-led ministry thrives?

Honestly, most churches answer a pragmatic no to this. They prefer a clean and ordered church to a messy nursery. But, again, as Tommy Tyson says, the new life is in the nursery. This is why Paul has to do so much teaching and correction on how to release and employ these gifts. He never hints at putting in controls to quench the gifts or restrict them to mature, trusted leaders. No, he states that everybody indeed gets to play—and play hard. There is no special priestly class. All are to be equipped, coached to their field positions and get into the game. Are we really ready for this? Do we build communities in which this is actually happening? Or is it really the anointed leader that counts, rather than the anointed Church? Does the leader do the ministry or equip the Church to do the ministry? How does this actually happen? How are we living this out? Is the pastor or priest a "player-coach" or the star? Are our eyes on Jesus and each other, or are they simply focused on the pastor? These questions have to be asked again and again.

Worship Enables the Spirit's Gifts to Be Given

Sixth, the Spirit's gifts or manifestations are given to be given. They are for the common good, to build up the body. They are not given to call attention to themselves or for personal power or gain. They are given to bless others and move us all into ministry.

As John Wimber taught, Spiritual gifts are also situational.[4] We are not talking about offices to fill in a church organizational plan. The gifts are released or passed out where the Spirit directs and the needs arise. Does someone need healing? The Spirit releases healing gifts. Does someone need encouragement? The Spirit releases gifts of exhortation and comfort. Does someone need money? The Spirit releases gifts of mercy and finances. Does someone need direction? The Spirit releases prophecy.

The gifts are to be expressed in an orderly way that actually builds up the church body. But order always is in tension with freedom (though not chaos). We need to remember that the Spirit is sovereign—we are to minister in reference to Him and to what He is doing. This will mean moments of silence, listening for His direction and, at times, shutting things down that don't build the body and aren't from Him. This will also mean moments of apparent chaos when He is moving dramatically upon people. Listen again to Paul:

> I thank God that I speak in tongues more than all of you. But in the church I would rather speak five intelligible words to instruct others than ten thousand words in a tongue. Brothers, stop thinking like children. In regard to evil be infants, but in your thinking be adults. So if the whole church comes together and everyone speaks in tongues, and some who do not understand or some unbelievers come in, will they not say that you are out of your mind? But if an unbeliever or someone who does not understand comes in while everybody is prophesying, he will be convinced by all that he is a sinner and will be judged by all, and the secrets of his heart will be laid bare. So he will fall down and worship God, exclaiming, "God is really among you!" (1 Cor. 14:18-20,23-25).

We need to ask, "When was the last time a 'sinner' fell down in our church and began to worship God, crying out that he is 'really among' us?" If this is not our current experience, why not? Where is the manifest presence of God?

As our worship ascends, the gifts descend; that is, they are poured out on the community so that we may be active in effective ministry. Sinners need to be converted. The sick need to be healed. The weak need to be strengthened. The demonized need to be delivered. The novices need to be grounded. We all need to hear a living Word from the Lord and grow in interdependence upon each other. "Your kingdom come, your will be done, on earth [right now] as it is in heaven."

Worship Is Motivated by Love

Finally, when Jesus is our effective Lord and the Spirit is sovereign, love motivates ministry: "Follow the way of love" (1 Cor. 14:1). As Paul says, if we have all the gifts, use them powerfully and create wonders, but lack love, all is emptiness and vanity (see 1 Cor. 13:1-3). The greatest acts of surrender and even martyrdom are nothing apart from love. But where the Father's love given in the Son fills us and empowers us, then the Spirit's gifts will be used properly. The Church will be built up rather than torn down. Christians will complement each other rather than compete with each other, and the power of God will bring Kingdom ministry right into our midst.

A COMMUNITY OF WORSHIP

Worship that is grounded in Jesus as Lord, filled with the Spirit, centered in the Cross (and its emblems in the Lord's Supper), engaging the whole Church, building the body with order and freedom, employing all the gifts and being driven by love needs to be expressed in small communities. Remember, the New Testament family was built by house churches. Both large and small congregations need to have smaller home groups that meet weekly. For in these groups, worship becomes intimate, relationships are built, teaching becomes interactive, and accountability and discipline are possible. In these smaller communities we can risk stepping out in prophetic gifts, learn to hear from the Lord and pray intensively (and long term) for healing.

John Wimber taught that we need to grow the Church "from the inside out." This means that lasting growth must come from building the infrastructure of small groups and ministry teams (for children, teens, men, women and those with special needs and interests). Consider Rock Harbor Church in Costa Mesa, California, which plateaued with about 2,000 people attending on the weekends. The church had as many people going out the back door as it had coming in the front door. Then the church launched a network of Life Groups that met weekly. Within two years, attendance on the weekends more than doubled.

Building small groups is cost effective. They need little or no budget, as they multiply ministry far beyond the professional staff. They become a key means of fulfilling Paul's vision for the Church to equip the saints for the work of ministry. Indeed, in these small groups, everybody gets to play.

The Church emerged in the Roman Empire through a network of house-churches or small groups. Christians worshiped together and shared their family life together. The Roman social class structure was breached as Jew and Greek, slave and free, male and female found each other as brothers and sisters in Christ (see Gal. 3:28). The Empire's moral, social, political and religious decay was reversed in these multiplying points of light. As it was then, so it is now.

The Kingdom is God's formula for healing the effects of divorce, abandonment, abuse and the ravages of addiction. The Kingdom is where the regeneration of marriage and family life is possible. In the Kingdom, aching loneliness is shattered as we are embraced by Christ and embrace each other.

Enter the Kingdom through the gate marked "Welcome Home!" You're in the Kingdom now.

POSTSCRIPT

Kingdom life begins in worship and ends in worship. Our destiny is to become eternal worshipers of the Triune God. When many hear this, they are turned off. They say, "I don't want to play a harp, sit on a cloud, or sing in a choir forever." They simply project their bad church experiences into their eternal future. But, as we have seen, worship, at its heart, is submission and surrender to the living God. It confesses, "Jesus Christ is Lord, to the glory of God the Father" (Phil. 2:11). True worshipers pray, "Your kingdom come, Your will be done on earth as it is in heaven." But one day this petition will turn to praise: "Your kingdom *has* come, Your will *is* done, right here, right now, on our transformed earth, throughout our transformed universe, as well as in the highest heaven."

While we live in the intersection of the Kingdom come and coming, one day we will pass into the Kingdom fully come. This will happen when the earth is evangelized; the gospel preached to every tongue, tribe and nation; and when Jesus appears visibly and gloriously in the clouds of heaven with His holy angels. Then the dead will be raised and the living transformed. They will be Christ's welcoming host as He comes to Earth to reign. Satan and his world ruler, Antichrist, will be defeated and cast into the lake of fire forever.

After the general resurrection, the nations will appear before Christ's judgment seat, where He will separate the sheep from the goats. The sheep will enter into His glory; the goats will be excluded forever (see Matt. 25:31-46). This will be the deepest punishment for them, the recognition of what they have missed. Then the kingdoms of this earth will fully become the kingdoms of our God and of His Christ—and He will reign forever and ever.

Although Christians disagree about the exact script for the final end times, it is vital to remember that we are not simply waiting for the end to come; we are already living in the end that began with the death and resurrection of Jesus. This prepares us for the judgment to come ("no condemnation"; see Rom. 8:1) and guarantees our own resurrection. Jack Hayford often says that he knows one thing for sure about the future: "He's coming and I'm going."[1] That's the essential point. We can differ when it comes to the details.

But what can we know of heaven, the fullness of the New Age, the Kingdom that we enter? C. S. Lewis offered the following thoughts: First, we will be with Christ. Second, we will be like Christ. Third, we will be glorified together with Christ. This means that we will be beautiful and praised. Fourth, we will feast and be entertained—it's eternal party time. Fifth, we will share with Christ in governing the new heaven and the new earth in which righteousness dwells.[2] Lewis missed only one further point: We will worship our brains out. Because we become like what we worship, we worship the living God because we will have become fully like Him.

We can only grasp dimly what this all means now. But we are grasped by Him: "Now we see but a poor reflection in a mirror; then we shall see face to face. Now I know in part; then I shall know fully, even as I am fully known" (1 Cor. 13:12). Until that day, we continue to share the Kingdom message and ministering of Jesus in the power of the Spirit. We continue to belong to His army of love and work to reclaim this planet fully for Him. We continue to belong to Christ and to each other, a community birthed and empowered by His Spirit, filled with vibrant worship, self-giving love, healing the sick, casting out demons and ministry to the poor and oppressed, taking captivity captive to the glory of God.

We are all a part of this as brothers and sisters in Christ. Rejoice! We are in the Kingdom now.

ENDNOTES

Chapter 1: What's Happened to Me?

1. Ronald Ruden, *The Craving Brain* (New York: HarperCollins, 1997), p. 11.
2. Allan Bloom, *The Closing of the American Mind* (New York: Simon and Schuster, 1987), p. 25.
3. C. S. Lewis, *Mere Christianity* (New York: Macmillan, 1953), p. 5.
4. John Dillenberger, ed., *Martin Luther: Selections from His Writings* (Garden City, NY: Anchor Books, 1961), p. 60.

Chapter 2: Delivered into God's Kingdom

1. See Karl Barth, *Evangelical Theology: An Introduction* (New York: Holt, Rinehart and Winston, 1963), Chapter 2, "The Word," pp. 15-25.
2. Gordon Fee, *Paul, the Spirit and the People of God* (Peabody, MA: Hendrickson, 1996), p. 95.

Chapter 3: "Here I Am to Worship"

1. See Don Williams, "Charismatic Worship," in Paul Basden, ed., *Exploring the Worship Spectrum* (Grand Rapids MI: Zondervan, 2004), pp. 142-143.
2. Tom Wright, *Bringing the Church to the World* (Minneapolis, MN: Bethany House, 1992), p. 51.
3. Martin Buber, *Israel and the World* (New York: Shocken Books, 1948), pp.14-16. See also Martin Buber, *I and Thou* (New York: Charles Scribners, 1937).
4. Dallas Willard, *The Divine Conspiracy* (San Francisco: HarperSanFrancisco, 1998), p. 12.
5. Don Williams, *12 Steps with Jesus* (Ventura CA: Regal, 2004), p. 79.

Chapter 4: Life in the Kingdom: Come on In!

1. See N. T. Wright, *The New Testament and the People of God* (Minneapolis, MN: Fortress Press, 1992), Chapter 10, "The Hope of Israel."
2. See N. T Wright, *Jesus and the Victory of God* (Minneapolis, MN: Fortress Press, 1996), pp. 160-162; George Ladd, *A Theology of the New Testament*, Revised Edition (Grand Rapids, MI: Eerdmans, 1993), p. 38.
3. Eberhard Bethge, *Dietrich Bonhoeffer* (New York: Harper and Row, 1970), p. 99.
4. Wright, *Jesus and the Victory of God*: "When his [Jesus'] commands to the demons were obeyed, there ought to be only one conclusion for the onlookers: Israel's god was at last becoming king. 'The kingdom of god has come upon you.' The battle was already joined, and it was the battle, not with Rome, but with the true accuser, satan," p. 453. [Note: Lower case letters for god and satan are in Wright's original text.]

5. See Ezekiel 37; Joel 2:28-29; Psalm 139:7-10. Compare Isaiah 11:1-3.

6. *A Treasury of A. W. Tozer* (Harrisburg, PA: Christian Publications, Inc., 1980): " . . . the doctrine of the Holy Spirit as held by evangelical Christians today has almost no practical value at all. In most Christian churches the Spirit is quite entirely overlooked. Whether He is present or absent makes no real difference to anyone," p. 40.

7. Rich Buhler, *Love: No Strings Attached* (Nashville, TN: Thomas Nelson, 1987), pp. 25.

8. See Romans 8:17; Ephesians 2:6; 1 Thessalonians 4:16-17; 2 Corinthians 3:18.

Chapter 5: Proclaim the Kingdom

1. George Eldon Ladd, *A Theology of the New Testament* (Grand Rapids, MI: William B. Eerdmans Publishing, 1993), chapter 6.

2. N. T. Wright, *The Challenge of Jesus* (Downers Grove, IL: InterVarsity Press, 1999), p. 27.

Chapter 6: Call to Kingdom Ministry

1. Dallas Willard, *The Divine Conspiracy* (San Francisco: HarperSanFrancisco, 1998), chapter 2.

2. *Ben Sirach* 6:36.

3. Dietrich Bonhoeffer, *The Cost of Discipleship* (New York: Macmillan Publishers, 1963), p. 61.

4. Louis Finkelstein, *Akiba* (New York: Covici Friede Publishers, 1936), p. 181.

Chapter 7: Release to the Captives

1. Martin Luther, "A Mighty Fortress Is Our God," third stanza.

2. Ramsay MacMullen, *Christianizing the Roman Empire: A.D. 100-400* (New Haven, CT: Yale University Press, 1984), n.p.

3. Irenaeus, *Irenaeus Against Heresies*, in *The Anti-Nicene Fathers* (Grand Rapids, MI: William B. Eerdmans, 1981), vol. 1, p. 409.

4. For a practical guide regarding this aspect of ministry, see Francis MacNutt, *Deliverance from Evil Spirits: A Practical Manual* (Grand Rapids, MI: Chosen Books, 1995).

Chapter 8: Healing the Sick

1. Carol Wimber, *John Wimber: The Way It Was* (London: Hodder and Stoughton, 1999), p. 135.

2. Bill Jackson, *The Quest for the Radical Middle: A History of the Vineyard* (Cape Town, South Africa: Vineyard International Publishing, 1999), p. 116.

3. Francis MacNutt, *Power to Heal* (Notre Dame, IN: Ave Maria Press, 1977), chapter 1.

Chapter 9: The Secret of Kingdom Ministry

1. David Aikman, *Jesus in Beijing* (Washington, DC: Regency Publishing, Inc., 2003), p. 7. *The World Christian Encyclopedia* estimates the number of Chinese Christians at 90 million. See Philip Jenkins, *The Next Christendom: The Coming of Global Christianity* (New York: Oxford Press, 2002), p. 223, note 3.

Chapter 10: Extending the Kingdom

1. N. T. Wright, *Jesus and the Victory of God* (Minneapolis, MN: Augsburg Fortress Press, 1997), p. 172.
2. N. T. Wright, *The Challenge of Jesus* (Downers Grove, IL: InterVarsity Press, 1999), p. 110.
3. Ibid., p. 120.
4. Tom Wright, *The Meal Jesus Gave Us* (Louisville, KY: Westminster John Knox Press, 1999), p. 50.

Chapter 11: Kingdom Surprise

1. Joachim Jeremias, *The Parables of Jesus* (New York: Scribner and Sons, 1955), p. 9.
2. N. T. Wright, *Jesus and the Victory of God* (Minneapolis, MN: Augsburg Fortress Press, 1997), p. 230.

Chapter 12: The Road Marked "Suffering"

1. Inscribed on Wesley's statue at the front of the Foundry Church in London, England.
2. C. S. Lewis, *The Problem of Pain* (New York: Macmillan Publishers, 1962), p. 93.
3. Francis MacNutt, *Power to Heal* (Notre Dame, IN: Ave Maria Press, 1977), p. 155.

Chapter 13: The Suffering King

1. Don Williams, *12 Steps with Jesus* (Ventura, CA: Regal Books, 2004), p. 48.
2. Gershen Kaufman, *Shame, the Power of Caring* (Cambridge, MA: Shenkman Publishing Company, 1980), quoted in John Bradshaw, *Bradshaw on the Family* (Deerfield Beach, FL: Health Communications, 1988), p. 2.
3. Bradshaw, *Bradshaw on the Family*, p. 2.
4. Ibid.
5. N. T. Wright, *The Challenge of Jesus* (Downer's Grove, IL: InterVarsity Press, 1999), p. 93.

Chapter 14: Kingdom Paradox: Death and Resurrection

1. N. T. Wright, *The Resurrection of the Son of God* (Minneapolis, MN: Augsburg Fortress Press, 2003), p. 31. For Wright, the key is not life after death but life after life after death, that is, resurrection life after going to heaven after death. He asserts, "The meaning of 'resurrection' as 'life *after* life after death' cannot be overemphasized."
2. Martin Hengel, *Crucifixion* (Philadelphia, PA: Augsburg Fortress Press, 1977), p. 7.
3. Ibid., pp. 41-42.

4. Ibid., p. 5.
5. Ibid., pp. 6-7.
6. Ibid., p. 10.
7. Ibid., p. 31.

Chapter 15: Kingdom Power

1. James D. G. Dunn, *Baptism in the Holy Spirit* (Naperville, IL: Alec R. Allenson Inc., 1970). "The high point in conversion-initiation is the gift of the Spirit," p. 4.
2. A. W. Tozer, *A Treasury of A. W. Tozer* (Harrisburg, PA: Christian Publications, Inc., 1980), p. 40.
3. Ibid., p. 56.
4. St. Irenaeus of Lyons, *Against Heresies* (Mahwah, NJ: Paulist Press, 1994), n.p.
5. Bede, *Ecclesiastical History of the English People* (London: Penguin Books, 1990), p. 52.
6. Ibid., p. 54.
7. Ibid., p. 68.
8. Ibid., p. 71.
9. Ibid., p. 93.
10. Wesley, *The Works of John Wesley* (Grand Rapids, MI: Baker Books, 1998), vols. 1-2, *Journal*, May 21, 1739.
11. Ibid., July 7, 1737.
12. Ibid., June 16, 1739.
13. Ibid., October 12, 1739.
14. Ibid., March 19 and 21, 1741.
15. Ibid., May 10, 1741.
16. Kevin Springer, ed., *Riding the Third Wave* (Basingstoke, Hants, England: Marshall Pickering, 1987), pp. 36-37.
17. Michael Cassidy, *Bursting the Wine Skins* (London: Hodder and Stoughton, 1983), p. 122.
18. Brother Yun and Paul Hattaway, *The Heavenly Man* (London: Monarch Books, 2002), p. 25.
19. Ibid., p. 26.
20. Ibid.
21. Ibid.
22. Ibid., p. 36.
23. Ibid., p. 49.

Chapter 16: Manifestations of the Spirit

1. Bill Jackson, *The Quest for the Radical Middle: A History of the Vineyard*, p. 61.
2. Ibid., p. 60.
3. Eifion Evans, *The Welsh Revival of 1904* (Bryntirion, Wales: Bryntirion Press, 1969), pp. 77-78.
4. Ibid.
5. Ibid.

Chapter 17: Persecution in the Kingdom

1. See N. T. Wright, *The Challenge of Jesus* (Downer's Grove, IL: InterVarsity Press, 1999), pp. 62-67. In *Bringing the Church to the World* (Minneapolis, MN: Bethany House Publishers, 1993), Wright states, "We can formulate the principle of the church's mission as follows: as Jesus to Israel, so the church to the world," p. 102.
2. David Bercot, ed., "Martyrs, Martyrdom," *A Dictionary of Early Christian Beliefs* (Peabody, MA: Hendrickson, 2002), p. 428.
3. Maxwell Staniforth, trans., *Early Christian Writings* (New York: Penguin Books, 1968), p. 105.
4. Bercot, *A Dictionary of Early Christian Beliefs*, p. 427.
5. John Wesley, *The Works of John Wesley* (Grand Rapids, MI: Baker Books, 1998), vols. 1-2, *Journal*, October 9, 1740.
6. Ibid., February 16, 1741.
7. Ibid., September 12, 1742.
8. Brother Yun and Paul Hattaway, *The Heavenly Man* (London: Monarch Books, 2002), p. 43.
9. Ibid.
10. Ibid., p. 46.
11. Ibid., p. 55.
12. Ibid., p. 56.
13. Ibid.
14. Ibid., pp. 56-57.

Chapter 18: Community of the King

1. John Bradshaw, *Bradshaw on the Family* (Deerfield Beach, FL: Health Communications, 1988), p. 4. "The crisis is far worse than anyone knows because the adults who parent their children were also abandoned and are separated from their own true inner selves. . . . So the crisis is not just about how we raise our children; it's about a hundred million people who look like adults, talk and dress like adults, but are actually adult children."
2. Anne Wilson Schaef, *Codependence: Misunderstood and Mistreated* (San Francisco: Harper and Row, 1986), p. 4.

Chapter 19: Relating in the Kingdom

1. See Luke 9:27; see also 2 Corinthians 4:10: literally, "the dying of Jesus" rather than "the death of Jesus."
2. A. W. Tozer, *A Treasury of A. W. Tozer* (Harrisburg, PA: Christian Publications, Inc., 1980), pp. 48-49.
3. Dietrich Bonhoeffer, *Life Together* (New York: Harper and Row, 1954), pp. 23-24.
4. Clyde S. Kilby, ed., *A Mind Awake: An Anthology of C. S. Lewis* (New York: Harcourt Brace Jovanovich, 1968), citation from Lewis's *The Four Loves*, p. 192.
5. From a personal conversation. Jamie pastors the Coast Vineyard Christian Fellowship in La Jolla, California.

6. Don Williams, *12 Steps with Jesus* (Ventura, CA: Regal Books, 2004), pp. 38-40. See also Mic Hunter, *Abused Boys: The Neglected Victims of Sexual Abuse* (New York: Fawcett Books, 1990), chapter 2, and John Bradshaw, *Bradshaw on the Family* (Deerfield Beach, FL: Health Communications, 1988), chapter 6.

Chapter 20: You're in the Kingdom Now

1. From a personal conversation.
2. D. Martyn Lloyd Jones, *Joy Unspeakable: The Baptism with the Holy* Spirit (Eastbourne, England: Kingsway Publications, 1984), pp. 18-19.
3. N. T. Wright, *The New Testament and the People of God* (Minneapolis, MN: Fortress Press, 1992), p. 362.
4. John Wimber and Kevin Springer, *Power Points* (San Francisco: HarperSanFrancisco, 1991), p. 147.

Postscript

1. From a personal conversation.
2. C. S. Lewis, *The Weight of Glory* (New York: Macmillan, 1962), pp. 3-19.

Get the Best-Selling Books About the Best-Seller Ever

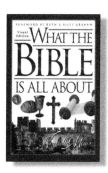
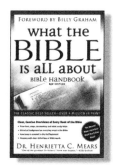
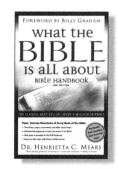
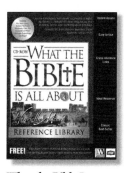
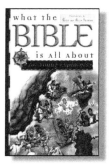
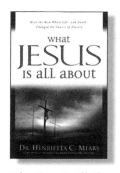

Make Your Daily Life Your Great Adventure

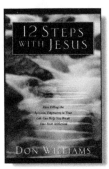

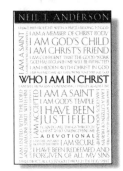

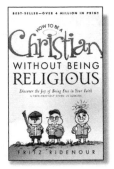